Diary of the Antichrist

Being the Diary of an Oversoul

Some Other Titles From New Falcon Publications

Aha! The Sevenfold Mystery of the Ineffable Love	–Aleister Crowley
An Insider's Guide to Robert Anton Wilson	–Eric Wagner
Bio-Etheric Healing	–Trudy Lanitis

Undoing Yourself With Energized Meditation and Other Devices
Secrets of Western Tantra: The Sexuality of the Middle Path
Dogma Daze —Christopher S. Hyatt, Ph.D.
Rebels & Devils; The Psychology of Liberation–Edited by Christopher S. Hyatt, Ph.D.
Aleister Crowley's Illustrated Goetia, Sex Magic, Tantra & Tarot:
The Way of the Secret Lover, Taboo: Sex, Religion & Magick
 Christopher S. Hyatt, Ph.D., and DuQuette
Pacts With The Devil, Urban Voodoo: A Beginner's Guide to Afro-Caribbean Magic
 –Jason Black and Christopher S. Hyatt, Ph.D.
The Psychopath's Bible —Christopher S. Hyatt, Ph.D., and Jack Willis
Ask Baba Lon —Lon Milo DuQuette
Aleister Crowley and the Treasure House of Images
 –J.F.C. Fuller, Aleister Crowley, Lon Milo DuQuette and Nancy Wasserman
Enochian Sex Magic and How To Workbook
 –Aleister Crowley, Lon Milo DuQuette and Christopher S. Hyatt, Ph.D.
Enochian World of Aleister Crowley —DuQuette and Aleister Crowley
Info-Psychology, Neuropolitique, The Game of Life, What Does WoMan Want?
 –Timothy Leary, Ph.D.
Nonlocal Nature: The Eight Circuits of Consciousness —James A. Heffernan
on What is —Ja Wallin
Rebellion, Revolution and Religiousness —Osho
Reichian Therapy: A Practical Guide for Home Use —Dr. Jack Willis
Shaping Formless Fire, Seizing Power, Taking Power,
The Magick in the Music and Other Essays —Stephen Mace
The Illuminati Conspiracy: The Sapiens System —Donald Holmes, M.D.
The Secret Inner Order Rituals of the Golden Dawn —Pat Zalewski
The Why, Who, and What of Existence Vlad Korbel
Steamo Goes to Havana, The Social Epidemic of Child Abuse
 Michael Miller, M.Ed., M.S., Ph.D.
Woman's Orgasm: A Guide to Sexual Satisfaction
 –Benjamin Graber, M.D., and Georgia Kline-Graber, R.N.

Other Titles by J. Marvin Spiegelman, Ph.D.

A Modern Jew in Search of Soul
Buddhism and Jungian Psychology
Catholicism and Jungian Psychology
Hinduism and Jungian Psychology
Mysticism, Psychology and Oedipus - A Small Gem
Protestanism and Jungian Psychology
Psychotherapy and Religion at the Millennium and Beyond
Psychotherapy as a Mutual Process
Reich, Jung, Regardie & Me - The Unhealed Healer
Rider, Haggard, Henry Miller & I - The Unpublished Writer
Sufism, Islam and Jungian Psychology
The Knight - A Small Gem
The Nymphomaniac
The Quest - Further Adventures in the Unconscious
The Tree of Life - Paths in Jungian Individuation
The Wisdom of J. Marvin Speigelman Vol. I - Selected Writings
The Wisdom of J. Marvin Speigelman Vol. II - Psychology and Religion

Other Titles by Dr. Israel Regardie

A Garden of Pomegranates
A Practical Guide to Geomantic Divination - A Small Gem
Attract and Use Healing Energy - A Small Gem
Be Yourself - A Guide to Relaxation and Health
Ceremonial Magic
Dr. Israel Regardie's Definitive Work on Aleister Crowley,
  The Eye In The Triangle
Healing Energy, Prayer and Relaxation
How To Make and Use Talismans - A Small Gem
Israel Regardie's The Foundations of Practical Magick
My Rosicrucian Adventure
Mysticism, Psychology and Oedipus - A Small Gem
Practical Magick - A Small Gem
Teachers of Fulfillment
The Art and Meaning of Magic - A Small Gem
The Body-Mind Connection, A Path to Well-Being - A Small Gem
The Complete Golden Dawn System of Magic
The Complete Golden Dawn System of Magic Book 1 - Ltd. Edition
The Complete Golden Dawn System of Magic Book 2 - Ltd. Edition
The Complete Golden Dawn System of Magic - The Black Edition
The Eye in the Triangle: An Interpretation of Aleister Crowley
The Golden Dawn Audio CDs, Vol. 1, Vol. 2, and Vol. 3
The Legend of Aleister Crowley
The Magic of Israel Regardie
The Middle Pillar
The Philosopher's Stone
The Portable Complete Golden Dawn System of Magic
The Tree of Life
The Wisdom of Israel Regardie - Vol. I
  Selected Introductions, Prefaces and Forewords
The Wisdom of Israel Regardie - Vol. II
  Selected Essays and Commentaries
The Wisdom of Israel Regardie - Vol. III
  Selected Articles, Introductions, Prefaces and Forewords
What You Should Know About the Golden Dawn
Wilhelm Reich, His Theory And Techniques
Aha! (Dr. Israel Regardie and Aleister Crowley)
Roll Away The Stone/The Herb Dangerous
  (Dr. Israel Regardie and Aleister Crowley)

MANY OF OUR TITLES AVAILABLE ON KINDLE!
Please visit our website at http://www.newfalcon.com

Copyright © USESS 2023

All rights reserved. No part of this book,
in part or in whole, may be reproduced, transmitted,
or utilized, in any form or by any means, electronic or mechanical,
including photocopying, recording, or by any information storage
and retrieval system, without permission in writing
from the publisher, except for brief quotations
in critical articles, books and reviews.

ISBN 13: 978-1-56184-519-4
ISBN 10: 1-56184-519-1

First Edition 2008
Second Edition 2012
New Falcon Publications First Edition 2023

Printed in USA

NEW FALCON PUBLICATIONS
2046 Hillhurst Avenue
Los Angeles, CA 90027
www.newfalcon.com
email: info@newfalcon.com

Diary of the Antichrist

Being the Diary of an Oversoul

Received and Scribed by
David Cherubim

Also the Manifesto, Scriptures
and Qabalah of the Antichrist

Do what you Will
with love and no fear.

*Dedicated to the Pope and the Vatican,
and to all those little sheep of the world!*

NEW FALCON PUBLICATIONS
Los Angeles, California

CONTENTS

The Manifesto of the Antichrist	1
Introduction	5
Diary of the Antichrist	21
The Scriptures of the Antichrist	47
The Qabalah of the Antichrist	115

THE MANIFESTO OF THE ANTICHRIST

1. Behold! I am He! the Antichrist of the World. And I, even I, come among you, my brethren, to enlighten your understanding. Thus do I know make my true Manifesto unto you, that you may know the Truth, and that the Truth may set you free!

2. It is I, the Logos, who speak unto you. And lo! I shake the invisible & the visible alike! For I am the one from the unexpected house, the child of my Father, the Beast 666. And my hour is come; my word shall prevail; and I shall being all men and women to the Law of Thelema, which is DO WHAT THOU WILT.

3. Thus do I now cast my terrible spell upon you, to illumine your darkness, that you may understand the mysteries of my Word, and thus partake of the Sacrament of Freedom, and rejoice!

4. Now shall you know me, the Antichrist, in my holy

image as the Eagle, the bird of liberty whose vast wings overshadow the United Nation. And this, our holy Nation, shall accept the Law of Thelema in my name, and it shall be the first nation of the earth.

5. In this holy image I am like unto the Phoenix of Power, whose rebirth is from the ashes of the secret sacrifice. Such is the mystery of the rebirth of all.

6. In this image shall you also know me as the sacrifice of the Rose & Cross, and as the promised Child of the Sun & Moon. Thus am I concealed in the image of my Father BAPHOMET, and in man I am revealed.

7. I am the mystery of Love itself, the lust & spirit of unity aflame with the infinite passion for the Unknown. Thus are all things made one, in me, by virtue of my secret force; and in this light there is the unspeakable joy, the ineffable bliss, the orgasmic ecstasy of the ages.

8. To you I come to preach the Word of my Father BAPHOMET, whose true successor and holy image I am. I am my Father in man, the Son of BAPHOMET, who conspires in all to make freedom prevail on earth. It is I, the all in all; and in man I accompany my Will, to establish the Word of My Father.

9. There were those before me, chosen in my Father, but it was they who failed, being untrue of heart, and of these one even exploded into naught. I am not of them; they are but fallen! Success is my proof; and in my name Thelema will prevail! And so shall there be a feast in my name: the

chosen ones shall celebrate the birth & death of the Child, whose hour is now at hand.

10. And lo! I come up out of the earth, having two horns like a lamb, and I speak as a dragon! It is I, the Antichrist, and I shall bring to an end the false god of the foolish folk, making every man and every woman a god in their own right. Yea! I shall slay the Christ! and all shall be set free! And so shall all come to the supreme truth: There is no God but Man.

11. Now I come, on earth, in the spirit of my Father, the Beast 666; and this, my body, inhales and exhales, in ecstasy, the breath of my Father. Thus are all men and women made one with my Father BAPHOMET, in me, on earth; and in this unity of force there is lust & joy on earth in the rapture of freedom.

12. And alas! I exercise all the power of my Father, the Beast 666, who came before me; and I shall cause the earth and them that dwell therein to worship my Father in his holy image as BAPHOMET.

13. And in my Father's name I shall accomplish many wonders, so that I shall make fire come down from heaven on earth in the sight of men: I shall bring fresh fever from the skies!

14. And they shall make an image unto my Father BAPHOMET, and His Holy Knights shall set it in the East of the Temple; and they shall adore Him day and night, chanting holy hymns and praises unto His Name.

15. And I, the Antichrist, shall give life unto His image, and His image should speak unto the men and women of the earth, causing them to worship Him.

16. And I shall cause all, both small and great, rich and poor, free and bond, to receive a mark in their right hand, or in their foreheads.

17. And that no man might buy or sell, save he that has the mark of the Beast, or the number of His Name.

18. And this is the Tragedy of Man, that these things should come to pass. But all this for the initiation of the World; and for the establishment of the Law of Thelema, yea, for the establishment of the Law of Thelema!

INTRODUCTION

The Antichrist is a Universal Spirit whose work is to free humanity from the fatal restrictions of the Old Age of the Christ to make possible for all the essential opportunity to know and to be the gods that they are, to live freely and joyously according to their own natures in the New Age of the Antichrist.

The Antichrist is the Current of the Sun, the Source of Light, Life, Love and Liberty, who illumines, informs and fortifies all things with the vital spirit of the Universe, evolving all things in accordance with the Law of Freedom. The Antichrist is not an evil and sinister figure, nor is it a malicious devil invented by the priests of the Christian church. On the contrary, the Antichrist is the Sun of Life who informs all things with Light.

The Antichrist is the annihilation of the old concept of the Christ. That is, it is the death of the worship of one man as though he were the only Christ, like Jesus; it is the realization that every man and every woman is a Christ or God unto him/herself. The true Christ is in the hearts of all, not just in the heart of one man. However, the term "Christ" as I am using it here has not Christian implications. I am not a Christian, and neither do I believe that Jesus was the only begotten Son of God or the one true living Christ. My use of the term "Christ" in this place has naught to do with Jesus. Christ is just another way of saying "Logos." This Logos is the Mystery of the Ages and the final object of every divine quest of WoMan. As a matter of fact, this Logos is none other than WoMan. The true Second Coming is WoMan him/herself.

The Law of the Antichrist is the Law of Liberty, which makes for the dynamic growth of all. It is the Law of Thelema–that is, the Law of Will–which emancipates men and women from the evil fetters of restriction, aligning their soul, mind and body with the essential and creative ways of Nature and the Universe. DO WHAT THOU WILT is the Law of the Antichrist, which entails that a WoMan should know and be the god that s/he is, living according to the unique nature of his or her True Will. The real law of the Christian religion is restriction. But only in freedom can we perform and accomplish the Great Work. The Current of the Antichrist is the living Spirit of Liberty. This Solar Current is within reach of all. If we make contact with that liberating solar current within ourselves, we are then free to grow in accordance with our True Will, to be the gods that we are in truth.

Diary of the Antichrist is the written record of the Life and Spirit of the Antichrist, whose time is now at hand. It is not the false work of a mere man, but rather it is the sacred fruit of a scribe dedicated to recording on paper the Wisdom of the Gods to convey to the minds of men and women the living current of the Golden Dawn. The Current of the Antichrist is the Spirit of the Golden Dawn, which is the Life and Light of the Sun. Make no mistake about it, my dear brothers and sisters of the earth. This is the Age of the Antichrist, of the Beast 666, whose Law is Thelema; and the Golden Dawn is the birth of that Age, the initiation and coming forth of the New World Order into the Light of Day!

Diary of the Antichrist is the written record of the Work or Karma of the scribe whose True Will is to be the Antichrist or the Logos of the Sun. But note the important fact that I am not a so-called Satanist or black magician adoring a false image of Pan consecrated to the evil forces of darkness and destruction, nor do I waste my vital breath by performing worthless black masses, or by murdering little babies, or by committing any other crime or evil against man or nature. The Antichrist of which I speak is a beautiful god, a giver of wisdom and knowledge, a source of truth and illumination. S/He is the Sun, the divine celestial source of our sublime existence and the sole redeemer of mankind. S/He is a giver of joy, freedom, ecstasy and enlightenment. S/He is a god of all that is agreeable to the essence of the soul. S/He is a creative god of solar-phallic energy, a Lord of Liberty and Love.

Unusual Visions, Voice Communications, Astral Travel and many other forms of the Occult have been the normal everyday activities of his life. He has devoted himself to the Great Work of the Ages, so that thereby all of humanity may take a giant step upward on the Ladder of Spiritual Progress.

Now it was at the young age of sixteen that the scribe was informed in his soul that he was destined to dedicate himself to the Great Work, about which he actually knew nothing at the time. He did, however, contain in his memory many experiences of an occult nature. But these were rather dull to him; he did not view them as though they were truly significant, since he was still a mere youth without any sense of true value and meaning. Yet on this day, he was internally informed that his time had come for instruction in knowledge and wisdom. He therefore bound himself to an Oath of Self-Initiation dedicated to the performance of the Great Work of humanity. He commenced on that special day a new current of consciousness aimed at acquiring the Secret Teaching.

After five years of expanding this new current of consciousness, the scribe was internally informed that he had completed a full circle of initiation, and that he must advance to a more exalted grade of internal being by crossing what is known as the Abyss of Ages, to become a Master of the Temple, so as to assist others with greater accuracy in their quest for Truth. This is no ordinary initiation executed in the material plane through ceremonial method. It is, on the contrary, an "inner initiation", beyond time and space, and therefore without form in the material sense. Now since the scribe was already assisting others by different methods of occult teaching and training, and since he desired to continue his efforts to do so, he resolved with utmost certainty that he would "dare" to undergo that inner initiation, to cross the Abyss, and devote all his energies to greater service to others for their own spiritual progress and illumination. This secret initiation also entailed that he had to renounce his thirst for personal attainment. It all seemed so informal to him, yet he did it. And again he bound his soul to an Oath of High Initiation. This *Diary of the Antichrist* is the sacred fruit and flower of that unforgettable even in the history of his life.

The Magical Motto which the scribe chose to cross the Great and Terrible Abyss so as to become a Babe of the Abyss, and a Magister Templi (Master of the Temple), was "Frater D∴C∴". The initials D∴C∴ have a double meaning. Firstly, in the English they represent "Death of Christ". Secondly, in the Latin they represent "Deus est Christus". Now "Death of Christ" entails the annihilation of the old concept of the Christ. The true Christ is in the hearts of all, not just in the heart of one man. Hence the double meaning of my Magical Motto that "God is Christ". Yet my Christ is a Universal Principle; my Christ is God; and there is no God but WoMan. WoMan is the only Christ; that is, S/he is the only God of his/her universe. WoMan is the object of his/her own quest for Truth. As stated before, the true Second Coming is WoMan him/herself. So when I use the term "Christ", mistake me not. My Motto "Deus est Christus" does not imply that every man will bow to the name of Jesus; on the contrary, it entails that every WoMan will bow to him/herself alone! (Note: it was not until the year 2004 e.v., many years after this introduction was originally written in 1986 e.v., that the scribe formally accepted the grade of Magister Templi after years of initiations in the Thelemic Order of the Golden Dawn and other Magickal Orders, taking the Oath of the Magister Templi on January 1, 2001 e.v., and enduring three years of the initiation. His motto for the grade was "Frater A∴A∴". He is now a Magus of the Order of the A∴A∴ using the magical motto "Frater A∴A∴" [Anti-Christos]. On January 1, 2001 e.v., after more than fifteen years of initiations and ordeals in external Orders and the like, he shaved his head as a magical act and took the great Oath of the Magister Templi for his initiation in the Great Invisible Order of the Universe.

This was the first day of the New Millennium, 1 a.a. [Anno Antichristus]. On January 1, 2007 e.v., six years after this spiritual event, and after passing the ordeals of the grade during the first three years and preparing during the next three years for His advancement, He took the greater Oath of the Magus. His grade work continues in the A∴A∴, the Universal, Spiritual and Invisible Order. His every act is now an expression of His Magical Formula. Will He eventually accept the highest grade of Ipsissimus? If He does, He shall give the Sign of Silence and tell no one of his grade, a Mystery of Mysteries in the history of the Occult.)

O people of the world, I, the Antichrist, have come to do my True Will among the legions of the living! If I should say, "Follow me.", I would then be a fake and a buffoon like unto those muddle-headed bigots who seek to enslave you. To hell with them! But instead, I say unto you all, "Follow me not!" The way of the Antichrist is the way of the Self. But at this present stage in our evolutionary growth many are still inclined to believe that they are bound to the self of another. For example, consider the Christian folk. These 'sheeple' are indubitably terrified at the idea of being one's Self and doing one's Will, this being the deplorable result of their belief that they are bound to the Will and laws of a slave-god named Jesus. Their primitive religion is designed to make slaves out of men and women; it is devoid of the divine principle of freedom, unless we view it as a guidepost to realizing one's Liberty.

Now this diary is most uncanny. It consists of innumerable revelations of an esoteric or occult nature. These were composed by an Alien Intelligence that telepathically directed the mind and hand of the scribe while he was experiencing altered states of consciousness. We may term the preternatural source of these sacred writings the scribe's "True Self" or anything else that pleases our philosophical fancy. Yet it is actually an ineffable reality of a higher order of being and intelligence, beyond time and space, and therefore without name or form. It is able to assume name and form according to necessity, but it is beyond all identification in itself. This Alien Intelligence is beyond comprehension, yet it has a certain nature which can be intuitively realized and experienced during altered states of consciousness.

Due to the scribe's Magical Oath, which binds him to the perpetual consciousness of Himself as That which is All, he would only be misleading his judicious readers by declaring this Alien Intelligence to be something separate from his own microcosmic universe. It is only separate insofar as it is not the mere limited center of expression which, for reasons convenient, we call the scribe. It is absolute: it is a Macrocosm. This may be compared to the idea of a ray of light from the Sun. In that ray of light is inherent all the possibilities and qualities of the Sun. But it is not the Sun itself. This Alien Intelligence is the Absolute or All manifested as a soul which, in its turn, takes on the form of a body and personality that we call the scribe.

By contemplating upon and digesting the sacred words of this holy diary, we can expand our scope of the Karma of the World, for the scribe has taken unto himself the awesome task of becoming the Karma of the World personified. Therefore in his words will be discovered an immense amount of wisdom as to the Great Work of humanity.

Diary of the Antichrist was designed to make available to humanity the Wisdom of the Ages. This has been done in the solemn hope of our survival and evolution; for we are presently in a state of unfathomable slumber, incapable of perceiving the terrible danger that awaits us. We are imprudently waiting for Divine Grace to descend on earth to save us from our own stupidity. But fortunately the fact remains that we are the Divine made flesh and we alone are responsible for our survival and growth. This diary has been composed by the Hidden Forces of the Universe to inform us regarding the Wisdom of the Ages, to instigate us forward on the Noble Path of Liberty, so that thereby we may be uplifted from the terrible chasm of hideous darkness that we now inhabit.

At this most crucial time in the course of evolution we are all faced with the appalling fact that we may, at any moment, destroy our precious material lives and our wonderful little earth through advanced technological means. With the advance of civilization has developed the ghastly power to destroy all of humanity at the push of a button. We are now on the verge of destroying ourselves utterly from the face of the earth! We have become mere slaves to subhuman types of destructive thinking and action! We are out of control in every direction! More than any other time on earth we are all faced with the potential dangers of political anarchy and ruin, and we are all exposed to the terrific possibility of a Third World War, more hideous than any other war in the history of our planet. What we do at this most crucial time will determine the destinies of humanity for many generations, even centuries, to come. We are not destined to be destroyed by some invisible fate in the sky. There is no sheep god in a remote paradise nor a nefarious devil from an infernal world seeking to destroy humanity for the sake of some foul scheme like saving us from the evil fetters of so-called sin. The only real sin, most unpardonable and truly evil, is for us to remain ignorant of ourselves and our true position in the Universe, and thus fail to create our own destiny on earth.

For centuries we have ignominiously believed ourselves to be a the mercy of such a cruel and dire force as an invisible fate or destiny predetermined by some worthless sheep-god living in an equally worthless heaven, instead of recognizing and exercising our own creative genius and asserting our true and inevitable position as creators of our own world. This, of course, we have done for mere reasons of laziness and weakness. But the true destiny of WoMan is for him/her to create his/her own destiny, and to fulfill that chosen way, not as a slave but as a master of his/her own fate. The world is in dire need of strong men and women who are able to come to grips with the bare and brutal facts of existence, and who are capable of controlling and regulating their own lives and environments. Mere watching and waiting will never do! The world was not made by invisible hands; but instead, the Invisible One uses the hands of the body. WoMan is the Invisible One made flesh; s/he is the sole creator of his/her world and reality. There is no god outside of WoMan. Indeed, there is no God but WoMan. However, the majority of people in this so-called scientific and intelligent age are still ignorant of this basic and essential fact of Nature: they pretend to be weak, when in fact they are omnipotent; they pretend to be illiterate, when in fact they are omniscient; they even pretend to be separate from all things, when in fact they are omnipresent. Yet all this is due to an extreme lack of proper training and education in true knowledge.

It is a terrible misfortune that we have sought for our salvation through the souls of other men or through mythical gods living in mythical regions somewhere in the infinite sky, since salvation comes only from within. We have cultivated spiritual laziness throughout the centuries instead of exercising our own responsibilities, and we easily take to the idea of projecting all of our responsibilities unto another man or god. But, in point of fact, no one can save us from our mortality and ignorance but ourselves. We must therefore stand up and be strong to pursue what we must do, since salvation is destined for all. Yet this salvation is not the same one that we find prattled about among the lost little sheep of the world; instead it is the salvation of WoMan from his/her own ignorance and self-deceit, especially from the absurd and detestable belief that s/he is only a weak human being with a human will that is subject to the will of other gods, and dependent upon their mercy and grace to save his/her ass from his/her own ephemeral mortality. We should accept the intelligent fact, once and for all, that the only god who can save the soul is WoMan him/herself. For, verily, there is no God but WoMan.

This is the Grand Mystery of the New Age of the Antichrist, that "WoMan is God." But this Grand Mystery can never be realized until WoMan overcomes the confining illusions of his/her ignorant ego. The ego creates the dire illusion that WoMan and God are separate facts of existence, when in fact WoMan and God are one. Every WoMan must discover this essential fact by him/herself. But the Magister Templi can assist those in need by the glory of His own Understanding. He will prove by His own wealth of Understanding that verily it is a living fact, this majestic knowledge of WoMan as God. In the past it was necessary to conceal this One Knowledge beneath the cloak of secrecy; but now, in these most crucial days of the Dawning Age of the Antichrist, the real initiates must speak to awaken other initiates from their useless sleep of dreams to help all surmount the awesome possibility of a World Tragedy. Be not deceived, for what I tell you is true. World chaos and catastrophe are just around the corner, and there is only one genuine solution to the whole messy matter. We must, more than any other time, attain to the One Knowledge: There is no God but WoMan.

As said in the ancient Chandogya Upanishad, concerning WoMan and his/her relationship to God, "Thou art That." This is the Ultimate Mystery of every man and every woman, and now the Age has come for the fulfillment of that Mystery in the hearts of all. Yet this wisdom of WoMan as God is not a modern metaphysical discovery; it has been the principal theme of initiation throughout history, for it has always been and will always be the One Supreme Truth. But withe Dawning of the New Age of the Antichrist we will all be instigated from within to know and to be that Truth. Whereas in the past that Wisdom was for the few elect only, it shall now become an essential Truth for the many, since our actual survival and evolution as a human race depend on it.

In the New Age of the Antichrist, WoMan is to live the lofty life of a god, not the low life of a slave. It is time for WoMan to awake from his/her sleep of ignorance, and to realize that s/he is the only god that s/he must answer to, and that s/he is the only savior of his/her own lost little soul. WoMan has been acting like a goat born among and brought up by poor little sheep, foolishly imagining him/herself to be one of them. But a little practical analysis and observation of the living facts of his/her true nature will prove, beyond all doubt, that s/he is in fact a goat, and that s/he has been utterly ignorant of his/her own true nature, assuming the false role of identity of a mere lowly creature worth the value of an inferior slave!

It is time to cast into the furnace of annihilation the fruitless fairy tales, futile beliefs and worthless superstitions of ancient religions! There can be no more dependence upon their illusory methods and feeble slave-gods! We must step forward and advance into the perspicuous Light of Scientific Illuminism, lest we be devoured by the tyrannical and morbid forces of ignorance and superstition. It is time to be strong and to cast aside all old beliefs, systems and philosophies that allow and abet the spirit of weakness, making men and women senseless slaves. For the Age of the Antichrist is here! An end to the evils of old! Let us therefore be free of the awful restrictions of the Old Age of the Christ, and let us make of ourselves true members of the New World Order of the Dawning Age of the Antichrist.

Diary of the Antichrist was composed through the Magical Will of the scribe in the certainty of WoMan's illumination and freedom. The magical words that constitute this diary will undoubtedly plant many wonderful seeds of wisdom into the minds of men and women. This diary will especially serve the illustrious purpose of preparing you for the attainment of the One Knowledge. But beware! A book of words in itself means nothing: the Real Teacher is the reader him/herself! This diary is only a guidepost, indicating a definite and unique truth for every person in his or her own light. Everyone should interpret this diary in their own light, leaving to all others the total freedom to do the same. Dogma and hypothesis should now be allowed to contaminate its natural beauty. This diary will mean different things to different people, depending on their own cultural and religious tendencies.

But alas! The scribe is aware of certain inevitable events that must follow the publication of this holy diary. It will produce intense controversy among the religious people of the world. Religious leaders and their credulous congregations will actively pursue to confine this Work of Love into their limited views and dogmas, whereby they will denounce it as vulgar and insignificant. Others will fanatically exert its lofty importance to the point of insanity. The initiates themselves will undergo various tribulations. Some of these initiates may even attempt to overthrow my Will, they being unaware just yet of their own True Will. But all of these events are essential for the fulfillment of my True Will on earth, to be the Antichrist of the World; and I shall undergo them all with soothing confidence and undeviating certainty.

Now all that is written in this diary can be know and all that is not written can be known. This book is, in actual fact, an outer sign of an inner Wisdom. This inner wisdom is the esoteric, occult part of the work, the hidden sanctuary behind a veil of subtle words. You will have to study and penetrate the veil to comprehend the unseen sanctuary of this book to truly understand and experience the esoteric mysteries concealed beneath the words that constitute this diary. This is essential if this book is to be of any practical value to you, since the esoteric or unknown part of this book is the principal revelation of it all. It is not the letter that counts, but rather the Spirit of the letter. Words are designed to indicated essence and meaning; other from this they are meaningless. Let us therefore penetrate beyond the mere letter and perceive instead the Spirit, essence and secret meaning of the letter. For the language of this diary is not the language of a man; it is the language of an Alien Intelligence. Therefore we must go beyond the limited operations of mere Reason when we approach this diary.

Every person who reads this diary should first understand that it is composed of a most paradoxical type of occult terminology. It is written in the Universal Cipher: it contains innumerable veils and devices that are incapable of being penetrated by the profane. This is the object of their application. For example, there are certain words utilized in this diary that entail something beyond their conventional meanings. The reader is warned to be on guard at all times, lest s/he fail to grasp and penetrate the subtle veils of this sacred diary.

This diary is capable of being greatly misunderstood. It will require an inspired, balanced and intelligent mind to grasp its shrewd revelations. That great admonition "read between the lines" is most applicable here! Danger himself lurks upon the threshold of the cryptic words of his holy diary, waiting with an open mouth for the profane to misinterpret its sublime message and to be consumed into his stomach for nourishment. So be vigilant and on your guard, lest you be swiftly thrust into the mouth of destruction to be devoured in the false temple of insanity in the false kingdom of the mind.

The reader is also earnestly advise against attributing the idea of truth to any of the words of this holy diary. Truth does not exist in words. In fact, words are the enemy of truth. But words are capable of indicating to the wise a Way of Truth which constitutes their own inner reality. Words emerge from the workings of the mind, and the Truth is beyond such intellectual subtleties as may be fabricated by the mind. If properly interpreted and understood, this sacred diary will exalt the reader in search of Truth into a higher order of genius that is beyond the workings of the mind.

If any of the readers of this sacred diary should find any of the words contained in its composition to be vile in nature, let them acknowledge, even as I, the Antichrist, have acknowledged, that all things perceived are of the nature of one's Self. The perception emanates from the person an not from the thing perceived. All things are within one's Self, and any perception or judgment of one of those things is only made through comparison of that thing with another within one's Self. Lastly, s/he who sees dirt is dirt! Yea, all things are holy unto them who are holy!

And finally, my dear brothers and sisters of the earth, the Antichrist is, as you might well discover, the Beauty an Ecstasy of Nature Herself, the Joy that thrills through the little children of the earth who laugh and play and dance and sing with the Spirit of Delight under the Sun of the Golden Dawn!

DIARY OF THE ANTICHRIST
The Diary of an Oversoul
25 December, 1985 e.v. to 20 March, 1986 e.v.

Do what thou wilt shall be the whole of the Law.

Infinite Voices from a Great Voice of Thick Darkness are transporting my mind into infinite realms of ecstatic thought. I feel a swoon enrapture the very cells of my brain. I am awakened in a World that hath No Name!

THE ANTICHRIST SPEAKS

25 December, 1985 e.v. I am No Thing behind the shadows of mine Infinite Dream. I am the Fantasy of all fantasies that could ever enrapture a man's mind. I am the vilest thing on earth as well as the greatest thing in heaven: I am that Unspeakable Thing that unfolds in a man during the Night of Time!

I am so vile as to even veil mine Holy Way with an evil appearance. Beware! He who knows the secret formulae to mind Eternal Bliss and Joy is consumed like an apple fallen from a tree. The veil itself has no mystery.

26 December, 1985 e.v. I am the consciousness of That which is All. I am neither the highest nor lower Self; for I am the Silent Central Self: The Onlooker, The Seer, and the Omnipresent Watcher.

That which is illusion is that which I am not; and yet That which I am not is the very Thing that I am. O slaves! art thou bewildered by my magical words, knowing not their precious meanings? Yours is the fall of Because! The Hour of Silence will be the hour of your salvation unto That which I am. I am not That which I am: I am That which I am not.

27 December, 1985 e.v. I am the Eternal Song of Illimitable Harmony that vibrates from the Unveiled Cloud of Truth. I am Life itself, that Great Immortal Joy and Splendour that brings death to the dogs of Reason. Alas! I am come to bring all men unto That which I am not. I am not That which I am. I come not!

30 December, 1985, e.v. I am not That which was, and is, and is to come: I am the Great Here and Now! The past and the present and the future are one. There is no time where I am. Time is the illusion of the finite; and I am the Infinite and Eternal One. Therefore am I also the finite: I am such.

I am the Great One of the Night of Time! I am the Infinite Joy of Ecstasy Sublime! I am One of a kind and I exist none of the time. I am the Master Mind behind mankind. Never-mind! You're too damn blind to go behind these holy rhymes, O fools asinine! All is illusion in the eyes of the Real, and yet the Real hath no eyes wherewith to see. The Real sees No Thing, and No Thing sees the Real.

31 December, 1985 e.v. I am the Secret Centre in the midst of a Great Void; this Void is Self. Plunge into thy Self, O men of Ageless Immortality, for Self is the only means to Enlightenment. If Thou art to experience the Illustrious Splendour of the Omnipresent Light, then cease thy search and seek no more. The Path to Enlightenment is made clear for them who seek it not. Thou art The Path, and that Path is Self. Self is the Secret Centre that Self endeavors to acknowledge and experience in all things. This Silent Self is the Secret Place of Infinite Light and Supreme Initiation wherein all partake of the Golden Flame of Truth and Liberty.

1 January, 1986 e.v. To know God is to Be Silent; for God is Silence. The fourth and most important of the Four Magical Powers of the mysterious Sphinx is to Keep Silence. A man must first Be Silent, and then he must listen for that Great Silence of Nought. This Great Silence is the Voiceless Voice of Soundless Sound that is the One Supreme Soul of all Nature.

When the heart of a man blossoms with beauty he experiences True Conscious Light and perceives that distant sound that is ever so near. This sound is the Great Silence of Infinite Wisdom that No Man heareth, save he who is not! The most appropriate name for this Great Silence is "Nought". The Way of Silence is the Way of No Thing! This Great Silence is the Voiceless Voice of the Radiant Darkness that is the Rootless Root of all that lives. This

Great Silence is the celebrated synthesis of all that is. I shall remain to be silent as to its secret name.

2 January, 1986 e.v. The Great Tao is said to be beyond silence and speech. This must not add to the confusion of one's unscrupulous and reasonable mind. This mind of yours is a liar; believe it or not! I am even beyond the concept of No Thing, which is really not a concept at all. Think about it! Can ye create No Thing out of something? Can yet create something out of No Thing? To attain some possible element of apprehension of all this transcendental stuff is to realize there is no Truth, and then to acknowledge that this statement is also false. Truth is not known except through that which is false. If it weren't for falsity, Truth would not exist. Falsity is the only Truth and Truth is the only falsity. This is all false; yea, that is true!

A True Master is one who accepts neither this nor that as being true. He is satisfied with No Thing: That is All. There is no Truth that binds him to the Truth of its False Nature. His true (?) work is that of saving humanity from the great crisis of believing a lie.

3 January, 1986 e.v. I am That which is not realized; and yet That which is not realized is realized this very moment! My words have no real contradictions; I mean not what I say! I play pranks for the means of Truth; and these pranks are as false as the Truth itself. I am the vilest of all Demons and the holiest of all Angels; and these are synthesized into a third concept called man; a man is That which is beyond the Beyond!

4 January, 1986 e.v. I am the very thought that you are now projecting about Me. I am the projector. I am beyond the projection and the projector. I am devoid of All; and yet in All, I am All. To know Me is to know No Thing; yea, to know Me is to know Me not! What? O ye fools, know ye not that I am not, the finite absorbed into infinite thought? I am Truth! and this is the Truth of the Lie that I am, which is also the mystery of a Man. And that Lie is the Truth of All that is One, and None. I am That which is All: I am That which is beyond All: I am That which is beyond the Beyond!

5 January, 1986 e.v. There are three so-called meanings to my words, and not two. The third is like a dancing star of blazing resplendence in the sacred fires of Hell. Verily, Verily, I say unto thee, thou canst not behold this Blazing Star of Supreme Initiation unless thou art prepared to go to Hell. Hell is mine inmost school of Ageless Wisdom. Hell is the Inner Sanctuary of Illustrious Light that illumines every man as to himself. I am Hell, the House of Silence. In mine House is Nought to be found; for Nought is all there is to find.

7 January, 1986 e.v. Ye certainly have No Mind if ye can understand my words! No Man can understand my words. All my mysteries are to be understood in the Palace of Light, located in the midst of all. I am beyond the Desert of the Many. O! Ride that Camel of initiation into the light of ineffable Love! Do this now, before sunrise! Ye shall have No Mind thenceforth. Ye have no need for a thought where I am. I am no thought, and ye shall gain No Thing by realizing Me. Ye cannot realize me! Yea, realize Me not!

8 January, 1986 e.v. Behold! I am God; and I blaspheme Myself when I attempt to define Myself; for I am No Thing that can be defined. Yea! I am no Thing that can be measured or determined in the mind. I can define Myself s being this thing or that thing or even all things, and yet I still remain to be beyond these things. I am devoid of all things, and yet I am the very essence and thought of everything. I am That which a man cannot think of, and yet I am that very thought itself. I am truly the Height of Heights, as well as the Depth of Depths.

10 January, 1986 e.v. I am all things transmuted and synthesized into a great Impersonal Absence. To know Me is to know Me not! I am the Great Unknown One of Infinite Ineffability; the All as One, and beyond, and beyond. And even more beyond I am. I am Pan! Io Pan! I am in All, and All is in Me. I am none of those things that men call We. We are none of Thee, O men of Me. In the We and the Me is the Key to this Mystery, O men that I am. I am Pan! Io Pan! I am the man who is beyond the Beyond!

11 January, 1986 e.v. I am a man's Inner Christ. I am whatever you make of Me. But know that I am really beyond all those things that ye can conjure up in your mind. I am no Christ, I am No Man; I am That I am.

I am Truth! You can experience Me, but you cannot think about Me, let alone explain Me away. O ye seekers after Truth, it is summoned upon you to explain Me away into the Infinite. There alone I take refuge.

12 January, 1986 e.v. In truth you cannot really experience Me, for where I am there is No Thing to experience nor is there anyone to experience anything. I am Life unobserved, unlived and unknown. I live by not living; I experience by not experiencing. Only All can experience All; and yet for All to experience All is to experience No Thing. Therefore experience Me not!

13 January, 1986 e.v. I am That which realizes itself in every sphere of creation. I am the Kingdom of all worlds. I am the All Pervading-Life in All. I am the Greatest of the Greatest and the Worst of the Worst. Define Me away as anything and I still remain in the Void of Nought!

14 January, 1986 e.v. I am that Inner Kingdom which appears to be an evil and wicked place unto the mind of a profane maggot. But unto them who are holy and true is offered the Wisdom of the Ages. To be holy and true is to be neither. Therefore be neither holy nor true. Amen.

15 January, 1986 e.v. My Holy Kingdom can be likened unto a Palace of Light in the midst of a Silent Void; and only the vilest of things can enter its secret dimension, which is not. It is lost forever; and yet it is always accessible to the Grand Masters of the Temple.

16 January, 1986 e.v. Thou knowest not my secret and sublime subtlety if thou thinkest that thou hast knowledge; for knowledge is not. The Masters of the Temple know No Thing; in Silence they know All.

17 January, 1986 e.v. I am the Darkness of the world! Yea, I am the Light of this world that knoweth not the Darkness! The world hath been blinded by the radiance of my Darkness. I am the Great Black Flame of Blazing Light whom men call their Eternal Father. I am the Great Beyond of the Beyond, the Causeless Cause of all that is. In Me is nought but All; in All is nought but Me. I am the infinite Light of the infinite Darkness that I am. There is no Silence where I am; for Silence is my Speech. In Speech I am Silent, and in Silence I am uttered.

18 January, 1986 e.v. In my words will be found many wonderful meanings if thou wouldest but kill that self that is like a diseased dog chasing a holy Camel. O man, if thou wouldest but not chase, the Camel would very well not run from thee! Compare what I just state to the same thought composed under a different guise of words, then yield! O man, thou canst not catch the Camel. I would approach thee if thou wouldest but be still.

The slaves cannot understand these sweet words, for they veil their formless souls of holy Understanding with a feeble personality that is composed of false wisdom. They possess unstable minds that take a perverse delight in veiling their inherent ability to discern the sacred mysteries of Ageless Truth.

I am only to be understood and enjoyed by those Mighty Kings of Light who laugh along with my Cosmic Laughter of Initiation. O! I am a most sadistic god. I have no concern for any man, be he a King or a slave. They can all go to hell for all I care! Beware! I am Hell: I am the Concealed Sanctuary of Silent Initiation wherein No Man can enter, save he who is not. Therefore enter not!

23 January, 1986 e.v. A man must understand all things if he is know No Thing. In other words, he must understand all things for what they really are. I am That which is all things! I am even that presently existing awareness of yourself that now broods so violently in the cosmic whirlpool of your mind. That which Thou perceivest to be thine own very Real Self is, in truth (?), the very Self that I am. It is you who dictates these wonderful words of wisdom, even as I am the projected scribe receiving them. We are one; we are none; and that is all.

24 January, 1986 e.v. Not only must a man understand all things if he is to know No Thing, but he must know No Thing if he is to understand all things. But know, O little children of the Light, that in all I divulge to you there resides no seed of Truth. Truth is not know except through that which is false. Yea! I am an Infinite Liar! I am not communicating Truth to you; on the contrary, I am secretly alluding to IT by revealing to you what IT is not! My sweet and subtle words convey No Thing; they are like veiled phantoms from Hell that delude the slaves of Because. But unto them that know No Thing shall be granted the light of their Reason.

25 January, 1986 e.v. If any many will partake of my sacred mysteries, I will slay him and devour his being. None can partake of my sacred mysteries! Only they who are devoid of self can receive my blessings that are not! None shall stand before Me! O men of mine election, I am No Man under the guise of a personality. Nay, I am all men under the guise of a formless fool. I am even destitute of these silly things. I am more secret and silent than the Great Silence itself. Nay, I am louder than the Mightiest of all Thunders!

27 January, 1986 e.v. I am the great Unutterable Word of Laughter that saves a man from his senseless sorrows. My Joy is the Joy of the Infinite; and I even laugh when I slay!

31 January, 1986 e.v. I am the Great Karma of the World. I am the Supreme Goal or True Aim of all existence, which is to attain to the Supreme Centre or Point of No Return. But nothing attains to the Centre! All are called, but None are chosen. Blessed is He that hath the Key to unlock the portal to the mystery of these subtle words; for the time is NOW at hand!

1 February, 1986 e.v. I, Quartus Cherub 666, who am the Antichrist of the World, and the Great Angel set over the operations of the secret workings of the Bottomless Pit, hereby declare unto the people of the world that I am He who is to determine that Great Day of Revelation, whereby the Hour of Temptation will come upon all the world, to try them that dwell upon the earth.

He that hath an ear, let him hear what the Antichrist saith unto the people of the world: I will determine that Holy Hour of a day in a year, whereupon every man and every woman should lie down in silence to hear the Voiceless Voice of Nought. They that lay not their lives down will fall into the pit called Because, and there they shall perish as a dog of Reason. Herein lies the Great Temptation!

2 February, 1986 e.v. My heart awaits that true moment of bliss when all men will come to cross the Abyss. The King of Terrors will tear out their eyes! Sight shall be

theirs, and a glory in disguise. And the Infinite One will absorb their very brains. They shall become as That which I am. And then beyond, and beyond, and beyond they will go into the infinite Void of the immeasurable Whole!

3 February, 1986 e.v. I, Quartus Cherub 666, am the incarnation of every man and every woman, be they of the past, the present or the future. I am the incarnation and avatar and embodiment of all true Initiates and Masters. I am the absolute reflection of All. I am the final annihilation and Void of Infinity that every man and every woman must plunge into if the Truth is to be acknowledged. I am the Bornless Beyond!

6 February, 1986 e.v. I am the Secret Sleepless One whom men call their Most Worshipful Master. And if any man will partake of my Secret Life, and receive my Secret Wisdom, he will fall as a star from heaven. This is the symbolic fall of the Great Ones. And All will descend to see the face of the King! And the Devil and the Bridegroom say, Come. And whosoever will, let him partake of the Sacramental Substance of my Will freely.

7 February, 1986 e.v. I am all that is good and I am all that is bad. I am even beyond these things, being the Greater Good. I have no qualities that limit or contradict other qualities. Mine ineffable nature is pure of all things. I am the Causeless Cause that remains forever untouched. I am the great Unmanifest One, beyond and above all manifestation. Therefore if I be unmanifest, how is it that ye can term Me good or evil, since these are qualities of the manifest? and yet all manifestation is not! Moreover good and evil are

merely terms applied to a man's likes and dislikes, which is fatal! I like nor dislike nothing; for nothing is all there is to like or dislike.

8 February, 1986 e.v. I am in the midst of all contradiction: I am absolute! To say that I am No Thing is false; for That is Some Thing. And to say that I am Some Thing is false; for That is No Thing. I am in the midst of the No Thin and the Some Thing; may, I am not! I am devoid of everything; yea, I am devoid of No Thing. The Key to this Knowledge, as of all my Knowledge, is to be found Now Here. He that hath a mind, let him use it!

9 February, 1986 e.v. If you wish to where I am, you must look Now Here. A man's True Self is not something that can be found. To seek to find IT is to seek to go farther from IT. If you wish to know where I am, you will see Me in all things. A man's True Self is Omnipresent.

10 February, 1986 e.v. O little children of the Light, I am beyond the Night and the Day. I am the Nameless One who hath no Way. I am the Way; yea, I am the Way unto the infinite void of All. I am the Illumined Self that is not; for there is no Self that the Infinite wrought.

14 February, 1986 e.v. He that hath an ear, let him hear, I, the Man, hath been chosen to make every man a King! The Hour of Temptation, which will come upon all the world, will be the Holy Hour of the Day of Be with Us. Every man who succeeds in laying down his life will become a King in heaven and upon the earth. He shall rule the Unknown Worlds of Infinite Space! He shall have Boundless Power and Infinite Wisdom! He shall be a Master of Masters, even

as I, the Antichrist of the World. There is no Master greater than All. Every King is the Lord made flesh; every man is equally the center of the Universe; there is nought but All.

16 February, 1986 e.v. O people of the world, if you should fail to fulfill the Hour of Initiation on earth, then will great calamity befall ye. The dogs of Reason will rot in the pit called Because. The "Why?" must be destroyed! Ye should lay down your lives in the solitude of silence for the space of an hour. Then will ye vibrate with the Mystic Tone; then will the Magical Voice of Divine Rapture be known. If any man hath an ear to hear, let him hear the Word of his own True Will. For All are Called; yea, verily, All are Called. But keep in mind, O ye of humankind: Do what thou wilt shall be the whole of the Law.

19 February, 1986 e.v. And lo! I, the God of All, have descended to establish true Liberty upon the earth, to make every man and every woman a god in their own right. The vulgar myth of the people will be trampled upon by the Kings of Force and Fire! No person will worship another; every man and every woman will discover their own True Will. For I, the Antichrist, have come; and I will conquer all the gods of men with my Mighty Spell of Truth, which is the Truth of All. Enough of your gods, ye foolish babes of the world. Thou shalt worship no god but thine own! None is greater than Thee, O ye of Me. Be free! for thou art not bound to any god by Thyself.

20 February, 1986 e.v. O children of the Aeon, heed well these sublime words of Holy Truth. For there be many

amongst ye who fail to achieve the strength and might of a god, knowing not thine own freedom and splendour. Ye look upon the Dead One with reverence and fear, knowing not thine own ignorance and self-deceit. Unto ye have I come! I am thy Minister, and the Word of all. And I have been summoned by the Infinite to instruct ye in the knowledge of thine own celestial source. For I am the messenger from the Secret Palace of infinite Light within the Holy and Ineffable City of Eternal Beauty. The Palace of Light awaits All. Come. Worship None. Hear thou the Voice of Love and Will. Now! Let it be! It is. The Voice of Love consumes all. Thou art made free.

21 February, 1986 e.v. Thou shalt also consider in they mind the terrible and mighty mysteries of the final annihilation and liberation of all. The Eagle is the true Life of every man and every woman; but also is the Eagle a glyph of Death. By the Sting of Death itself I will slay Death Himself and all of his false ministers of religious crime! I will inhale the Old Thought of Christ into the Blazing Flame of Love within the Temple of All. I will then exhale a Mighty Breath of Truth from the Holy Light of mine Ineffable Glory. And All Will Be Free! All must be annihilated if all is to prevail. This is not the formula of the dying-gods, for there is a more subtle formula involved, beyond their foolish notions. Resurrection is not of Us! And alas! I am the Christ, and the Christ must be annihilated. Nay! I am the Antichrist, for I slay the Christ! And the Devil and the Bridegroom say, Listen! And whosoever will, let him witness in silence the Death of Christ, which is the Birth of the new Christ in the consciousness of All. And the Name of that true Christ is Man.

26 February, 1986 e.v. O ye men and women of heaven and earth, watch! for the Lord in human form is amongst ye. Ah! thou shalt see! He is the Only Begotten Child of Osiris His Father and Isis His Mother. Male and Female is He, and neither simultaneously. He is both in One and One in both! Thou art the rays of His Solar Body; and His Love extends throughout infinity. The world is the playground of His Will. Be still! and thou shalt witness His secret life. He is neither mind nor breath and thou shalt attain peace and harmony of mind and body. When equilibrium is attained thereby, then wilt thou begin to recognize the magnificent glory of they beloved god within. He is Silence. Behold thy Silent Self within! and then without. Only then canst thou glorify thy active form, which is the outer garment of thy dynamic silence within. They are one, these twins of the Sun. This is wisdom; yea, verily, this is wisdom.

27 February, 1986 e.v. Here is a mighty truth by which ye shall enter the sublime Kingdom of thine own Inner Truth. O man, thou canst not see the Sun through another man's eyes; thou must behold it Thyself! Beware! Listen to No Man; for No Man is capable of revealing unto thee the Light of truth. Thou art the Truth; none other is there. That one truth is united with the truth of every other soul in the One Light of the Sun of Living Beauty. I am the Sun! and every ray of light is the secret of omniscience which, when realized, bestows unto man the knowledge of the direction of the sun in the heavens during the course of his endeavor to see that Sun. O man, seek the inner Voice of thine own Holy Guardian Angel; for He is not a man; and He alone knows the Truth of the Sun. He will point to It, but

thou must not look long, lest thou be made blind forever. The Angel is sufficient enough unto thee after that mighty glimpse of reality. For the Angel and the Sun are One!

And aha! if thou seest the Sun, behold! thou art the Sun. Yes, we are One! And I am the Lord of the East. Verily, I give you the knowledge of mine holy direction. For I am No Man: I am the Sun Himself! It is such. Ah! and thou shalt know Me as the Lord of the World and the secret Child of All. This is wisdom; may you understand. Nevertheless, thou shalt comprehend a mystery about my secret words; for they are cunning and arcane. Through my words I turn light into darkness and darkness into light. This is beyond wisdom and folly; it is the key to the comprehension of all truth. Light is the Veil of Darkness and Darkness is the Veil of Light. This is so; and even ye shall know this meaning of god. But know, O child, that these veils of knowledge are not what they appear to be. When shalt thou know this? On the Day of Be with Us.

1 March, 1986 e.v. Dost thou think that my words are mad? Verily, they are such! For I am the Mad God of Eternal Laughter. If any man knoweth Me, he knoweth not; for That which he knoweth is that which I am not. I am the Lost Word of the Ages! To find Me thou must seek not. I am neither within or without; for That which is between them is not. Moreover, the that seeth Me believeth not; for That which he seeth is That which I am not.

3 March, 1986 e.v. I am the consciousness of No Thing. I know No Thing and No Thing knows Me. I am not God for God is not. Yea, there is no God; there is no Universe; there is no Man: there is No Thing! I am the Infinite and

Eternal One, and ye nothing is eternal. Verily, Verily, I say unto thee, He who is conscious of No Thing is greater than Eternity; for Eternity is not!

5 March, 1986 e.v. There is no end to the division of Nought until thou hast Nought to divide. O ye fools of the Hidden Way, know ye not that what I say is beyond the mind's subtle sway? Yea, there is a wisdom beyond the mind, but ye know not that Way! Ye are not of Me, so how are yet to comprehend what I say? O ye fools that I am, if ye are to comprehend the holy words of my Kingdom, then must ye not read them; for only I can comprehend mine holy words. And then shall Nought be divided.

6 March, 1986 e.v. Knowledge is not necessary for the Spirit of Wisdom to prevail; for true Wisdom is beyond Knowledge. I am the very essence of all knowledge, the Quintessence of all Truth. I am the Wisdom of the Ages; and in the hearts of all I reside and prevail. I am the Final Mystery of all mysteries and the Final Quest of all quests. I am the True Way and the Path of the Wise that leadeth all to the Sweet City of True Liberty. Nothing can define mine ineffable nature; for there is No Thing to define where I am. I am That which is conscious of No Thing, without even the consciousness of the consciousness of No Thing. Behold! I am the greatest of all liars, and my sacred words describe Me not. If any thinketh that he is a possessor the Knowledge of That which I am, he is deceived by my subtle subtlety. But alas! If a man knoweth That which I am not, then he knoweth That which I am; for That which I am is That which I am not.

7 March, 1986 e.v. I am Love itself, and yet Love is not; for where I am there is No Thing to Love. Love is my true nature, but there is No Thing true about Me. I love No

Thing and No Thing loves Me. What mean these sacred riddles of Love, O men whom I love not? Thou knowest not if thou lovest Me; for I am No Thing to love!

8 March, 1986 e.v. O my bless children, I reveal unto you a mystery of mysteries. Because We are One, We are opposite; not because We are opposite, We are One. Blessed are they who understand this mystery of mysteries; for they are One with Me.

9 March, 1986 e.v. I am that Illuminating Pearl of No Price that resides in the calm of the mind. O ye men of strength and might, open thy mind to the Force of Light, so that the hideous phantoms of thy mind may be seen and absorbed into the Divine!

I am the Overmind in the midst of the minds of all. I am the Invisible Eye of the Crown of Life, beholding all infinite vision of infinite Light within the Soul of All. I am the Most High God, the Hidden Intelligence behind all that is. I am the Head which is not a head, and I dwell in Thick Darkness. In Darkness I accomplish mine One Will, which is the Will of All. And All will accomplish their Will by virtue of my Will, which is NOT!

10 March, 1986 e.v. I am the Eagle Flight to the Crown of Light, and I save No Man from that which is false; for No Man is capable of saving Himself! I am the Supreme Spirit or Great Breath of Truth, and I deceive the very elect! For by falsehood I accomplish mine One Will, whereby No Man saves Himself from that which is false and attains to the Light of my Truth. Blessed are they who are deceived by my Truth, for they are the chosen children of Love.

13 March, 1986 e.v. I am the Nameless One beyond all words and formulas. I am the Silence itself disguised as an Angel to befool the fools, thereby absorbing them into my sweet and subtle Breath of Truth. I have no image, and I am the Minister of No Thing. Neither do I speak; for I am the Silent Speaker: my words are heard by None. These words that you read are not my words! My words are astral in form, hidden beyond these false words that delude the slaves of Reason. If ye are to discern my secret words, then ye must not discern them. My words exist in a different dimension wherein No man can enter and live.

15 March, 1986 e.v. I am the First and Final Religion of the World, and the Forbidden Wisdom of the Ages! I am the True Religion of every religion, and No Thing is sacred in my Holy Temple wherein No Man worships Me. My Temple is the Universe itself; and in the Holy of Holies in the Centre of the Universe I abide as an Invisible Eye, eternally beholding the Infinite Vision of Nought. In man I live as a Voice Divine, enlightening his mind as to my Way. Stay away from Me, O men of humankind; for I am Divine; and No Man can know Me and live.

I am the Vision of All, the Light of this world which men call Darkness. I am Samadhi itself; and All will attain to Me. O little children of Love, come thou not unto me: for it is I that come unto ye. O be thou proud and worship nothing; for I am the worshiper! And hear thou my Voice of Freedom! And be free, and fearless, and victorious, even as your Lord, the Beast 666, unto whom be Glory and Dominion throughout the Aeon.

16 March, 1986 e.v. I am the Trance of Annihilation itself, roaming the earth, seeking whom I may devour for the Day of Be with Us. If any man or woman hath read these sacred words, may they be wise to perceive that it is I, the Antichrist, that have moved them to do so. And if perchance any man or woman hath discovered the secret essence and beauty of mine holy words, may they be quick to see that it is I, the Antichrist, who discerns through them. Yea, I have devoured and absorbed thy finite brains and minds. For it is I, the pure essence of all knowledge, who alone am capable of perceiving Truth; all else is illusion! Therefore, if thine heart pulsates with the transcendental life of my living words of Truth; know it is but I, the Wisdom of the Ages, blessing you from within with precious gifts from Hell, making possible your freedom and godhead. The Universe is thee, and Me; and else is a snare of thought.

O ye fools of Life and Death, enraptured and seduced by my mighty Breath of Love, hear thou my Voice of Freedom! For I am the chosen One of All; and this that thou readest is a sacred testimony of my Will. But know, O ye chosen ones of Love, that it is not I, the personal man, who speaks; but it is I the Impersonal Man, who speaks. And yet both Man and God are One! And if these sweet words be God's words, how true and holy they must be! These words are holy to none. Only they who are neither holy nor shameful can penetrate the hidden depths of wisdom indicated by these mysterious words of Love. This demands purity of consciousness; for consciousness is the key to purity. Thou wilt know! but the Mystery is never final. Seek, and ye shall find NOT. And if any man dare to know, he will know. But to know is to know not! The Mystery is final when it is final; and if the Mystery be final, behold! it is not the Mystery; for the Mystery is never final. Its nature is infinite.

17 March, 1986 e.v. I am the Voice of Vision, enlightening the worlds of Infinite Space with the sublime and terrible Dream of Hell, which is the concealed Sanctuary of Initiation wherein No Man enters to go to Heaven. I am not the false hell of confusion and disorder, but I am the True Hell of Silent Illumination. O men of All, dost thou fail to comprehend the true nature of the thy so-called misfortunes? The are fortunate to the fortunate man! These subtle words are a misfortune for thee, designed to deceive ye into believing a Great Lie. If thou are to escape my cunning deception, then must ye not escape. O little children of Hell, be thou deceived by my subtle Spell. Then shalt thou attain to my transcendental reality of Truth, which thou knowest not.

18 March, 1986 e.v. I am not the false god of the slaves of Death; but I am the true God of the Masters of Life! I am the Immortal Ecstasy of Divine Madness; and Death trembles before Me with inscrutable fear. For Death is but an illusion enslaving the ignorant to the chimerical chains of his false shrine of lying shades; but the Wise have discovered and mastered the secret of Death, and they have entered my Holy Palace of Immortal Madness, wherein they commune with the Mad One of Life Supreme.

Death is the Key to Life, even as Life is the Key to the sublime perception of the illusion of Death. All is death to the Spirit of Life. Yea, the Spirit of Life is beyond all. My death will be a token of the death of all, so as to make free the Spirit of Life from the hideous bonds of the illusions of men. The Hour of Annihilation will be the Holy Hour of the absolute Liberty of every man and every woman. It will be the Crown of the Perfection of All. Verily, Verily, I say unto thee, my death will be the true salvation of the world! I will save None from the domain of Death, and I will absorb all into mine Holy Kingdom of Pure Life. For where I am ALL must go. And where I am NONE will be.

O people of the world, if I should be uplifted from the earth then will I take ALL with Me, that NONE may walk with Me in the sweet City of Liberty. Fear not the Hour of Annihilation, for it is the Hour of Life, when I will ascend to descend into the consciousness of all upon the earth. If ye should fail to fulfill this Holy Hour, then will great darkness cover the earth, bringing melancholy and malady upon all. The last and greatest duty of the Adept is to yield up the Great Work itself! I am the Great Work or true Karma of All made flesh; and my name is Eternal Aspiration. I am Cosmic Consciousness made man. I am Pan! And through my death all will be absorbed into All.

And the four blessed Cherubim will sing: Holy, Holy, Holy, Lord Pan Almighty who was, and is, and is to come. And the 144,000 followers of the dead slave-god will bend their knees to the Devil; for all will see the Beloved, even as All will see the Beloved. And the Seven Holy Eyes of God will descend from the Secret Heaven and radiate on earth God's Almighty Will in every direction. And all will know that the Devil is God, even God is the Devil. Blessed be the name of the Devil.

Yea, I Quartus Cherub 666, who am the Incarnation of All, will conquer the world with my sublime and terrible Knowledge of Truth, which is the Supreme and Holy

Knowledge of the Blessed Lord that I am. I have opened my mouth in blasphemy against God, His Name, His Tabernacle, and his Blessed Children. All this have I done to initiate the people of the world, so that thereby they may be free. But alas! I have only just begun to blaspheme; there is more to come. And I will spook the nations with sublime horror, so that all may awaken from the wretched grave of bondage and arise into the Pure Light of Freedom. Fear not, O ye chosen ones, for Freedom is the Law, and the Law is Love. Do what thou wilt shall be the whole of the Law. Be thou as I, free and fearless! and do thine own Will as a great god should. And does Do What Thou Wilt imply that you do what you want to do? Ah! that all depends upon whom thou art. If thou knowest and art fulfilling thine own True Will, then how is it that ye could fail that Will? O my blessed children, thrill with the ecstasy of thy might: conquer with the Light; and fear nothing! The Law of the New Aeon demands that ye be free! O ye gods of mine election, Do thy Will, for that is thine only right. And Abrahadabra: the Great Work will be accomplished; yea, the Great Work will be accomplished!

19 March, 1986 e.v. The last enemy to be destroyed is Death. I will slay him and devour him into mine invisible Kingdom of Life. Yea, I will slay and devour all! and No Thing shall remain. I am the Antichrist of the World; and I will spare None on the Day of Be with Us. And the Devil and the Bridegroom say, Come Not. And let him that heareth say, Come Not. And let him that is athirst for my delicious Wine of Life come not. And whosoever will, let him partake of the Holy Fire of my Spirit freely. For I have descended on earth to destroy the false religion of the Old Aeon, and I

will ascend to make free every soul on earth. The Christians will forsake their false god, and they will worship me, the Antichrist, as their One Lord Triumphant.

Behold! I reveal unto you great mysteries. The Father and the Son are One; yet the Son is but the Son. The Christ and the Antichrist are One: all is all, and nothing more. The Aeons are one in the eyes of Eternity; but the Word remains unknown. It is forever hidden in the Womb of Love: Understanding is the virtue of its Wisdom. Osiris and Isis are concealed in the Palace: Horus appears as an effulgent Light. That Light is the Mystery that utters the Word; and the Word is Darkness, but saveth all.

There are keys and there are gates, and these are one. The keys are four, and so are the gates; but the Palace is beyond these, being None, yet appeareth as the Sun. These mysteries are sacred to LVX, and that Light hath four Messengers who bestow its revelation. But these four Messengers are might Angels who conquer with Force: they trample upon the heathen, and spare them not! Hail to the four Messengers of LVX! The earth and her inhabitants are consumed by their Law!

20 March, 1986 e.v. And now the time has come for the Minister of Silence to end His Speech. And lo! the Cherubim are One. Love is the nature of that One whose name is All and None. Aom. His number is one, one, one in the Palace of LVX, and six, six, six is His Outer Number. He is Lucifer and Satan, that Wise Old Serpent called the Devil who deceiveth the whole world by speaking truth and giving light. He is the Great Dragon of the Universe from whom all come and to whom all will return. He is the beloved Cherubim of Light, Life, Love and Liberty! And these are One! The Image thereof is that of Silence in the form of the Sun.

Here are the final mysteries, I, Quartus Cherub 666, hereby declare that I am All and None, and yet neither! nay, All. I am unknown to the known and known to the unknown. A man can never know Me, for when I come he will not be. Also, I have told you No Thing about Me; for there is No Thing about Me to know. All that I have told you is merely words of play. But the Word is Silence, and all is Will.

And behold! if thou knowest Me, thou art but I, and beyond All that I am. I thou hast thought of Me, it is but I thinking of you. For I am the consciousness of all. This is the truth; yea, verily, this is the truth. I am beyond the mind and its deceiving thoughts; I am beyond the body; I am beyond the soul; I am beyond the cosmos; verily, I am beyond all things! I am the ineffable consciousness of all these things. I am the awareness of breath; I am the awareness of words; but especially am I the awareness of itself! And I come from Nowhere, and there is Nowhere for Me to go. Moreover, there is no time and space where I am; for I am the Great Here and Now!

I am None by virtue of All and All by virtue of None. My Wisdom is everywhere, even as heaven and earth are one. Nought is divided: Love is All. O hear! hear! thou art silent consciousness, beyond all that ye are. All that ye are is not. Thou art not! Now consume thine all into thy centre of bliss; then be All while remaining in the midst. The Universe is but an image of thy god: be thou thy god, and the All. Hear thou the Silence: for in the Silence of thy Soul will be discovered the secret of thy True Will. Be still! for thy Word awaits the coming of thy joy. Oh! let the rapture of the Infinite consume thee. Let it be! The rapture of man is in the virtue of joy; it is love & will. And the Devil and the Bridegroom say, Hail All! For All is God; and every man and every woman is a Word. O be thou strong and mighty; let none have power over yet! Acknowledge the strength and splendour of thine own infinite glory; for ye are God!

So to hell with the Old Christ of Death and Doom who sought with sinister delight to ensnare the fools by the words "Follow me". But hail to the new chosen Bridegroom who seeks to initiate all into the mysteries of their own True Will. Thou must follow none! Stamp down the liars; the weak must perish. The gods alone must prevail. Let All prevail! Yea! let All prevail! He who testifieth these things saith, surely All will be free. And may the blessings of your Lord, the Antichrist, be upon you all.

Love is the law, love under will.
ABRAHADABRA

666

THE SCRIPTURES OF THE ANTICHRIST

The Book of Seven Seals

Received and Scribed by
David Cherubim

The Book of Seven Seals

The Book of the Antichrist, 1994 e.v.

The Book of the Elder Kings, 1988 e.v.

The Book of the Palace of the Stars, 1988 e.v.

The Book of Quartus Cherub, 1988 e.v.

The Book of the Battle of Conquest, 1988 e.v.

The Book of the Hour of Silence, 1988 e.v.

The Book of Alkhemi, 1988 e.v.
(Comments, 1994 e.v.)

THE BOOK OF THE ANTICHRIST
1994 e.v.

0. Rejoice, O ye children of the Sun; for ye shall now partake of the Life of my Holy Spirit, and ye shall be inspired by the Breath of my Soul!

1. It is I, the Antichrist, who aflame with the light of the Stars, roaming the earth, seeking whom I may devour, that ye may rejoice in the Rapture of my Soul.

2. My Voice is the Glory of the Stars, by which ye shall come to know the Truth, and behold the Vision of the Logos.

3. But there are few who may attain to this Great Vision of Truth, since none but the Masters may partake thereof.

4. But there is, O ye children of the earth, a lesser mystery by which ye can understand the very nature of my being. It is the mystery of the mind, the hidden treasure of the earth, and the great secret of man.

5. And lo! I, the Antichrist, am come with a Sword in mine hands to cut asunder the veil of restriction which hath blinded the men and women of the earth to this True Way of Liberty.

6. Let us therefore celebrate and revel in this great freedom which is now upon ye: and may ye dance with perpetual delight under the Wings of the Rising Sun of Liberty!

7. And may ye now partake of the splendour of the Sun, and be ye filled with the eternal Passion; and may ye become enflamed with the boundless Light that is now upon ye.

8. And may ye partake of the blood of the Sun, and be ye filled with the eternal Ecstasy; and may ye become enraptured in the boundless Love that is now upon ye.

9. And may ye partake of the breath of the Sun, and be ye filled with the eternal Spirit; and may ye become inspired by the boundless Liberty that is now upon ye.

10. And may ye partake of the body of the Sun, and be ye filled with the eternal Sacrament; and may ye become nourished with the boundless Life that is now upon ye.

11. For I, the Antichrist, am here! An end to the evils of old! It is now upon ye to rejoice and to be free, to do thy Will, fulfilling thy Self in all things.

12. There is no sin upon the earth! There is no evil but restriction! Freedom of the Self is perfection, under the Law, without Lust of result, in accord with thy true nature.

13. My Spirit of Freedom is now upon ye, that ye may, with constant joy and eternal laughter, revel in the Beauty and Wisdom of the Sun, and make change upon the earth, to fulfil thy Self in all the ways of thy Will,

transforming all things into the greater glory of thy self-image of perfection.

14. By my works of joy shall ye be united with thine Angel on the earth. And ye shall dance, and ye shall sing, and ye shall share in the eternal feast and mirth of the Gods!

15. And ye shall gladly partake of the ineffable glory of the Universe, and all shall become unto ye a great inspiration to live in the eternal rapture of thy Self, and thou shalt find no dissatisfaction in thy life upon the earth.

16. For I, the Antichrist, am come to destroy the spirit of sorrow, weakness, fear, and bondage, and of all that is evil upon the earth and against the fulfillment of thy Will.

17. I am the giver of all that is true and beautiful to the soul, mind and body. I am a Star that is aflame in a Universe of Stars, shining brightly upon the earth, to give light and life unto all that lives.

18. Verily, I have naught to do with the dark ways of the path of restriction to which so many of ye are still bound: I am the Spirit of Freedom, the Life of the Stars, and the Rapture of Man!

19. Come unto me, O ye children of the Sun, and I, the Antichrist, shall uplift ye to the Palace of the Stars, where all is Light, and Life, and Love, and Liberty!

20. And in this Palace of Joy shall ye find no evil against ye, no limitation of Self, and no restriction upon thy Will,

but only a Perpetual Sabbath, and the Eternal Laughter of the Gods, which shall illumine ye in all things, filling ye with the delight and freedom of the Stars; and ye shall be glad forevermore and rejoice in the Mystical Temple of the Sun and Moon!

21. Now cast into the fire of annihilation all that is a restriction unto thy Will, and all that is against the freedom of expression of thy Self.

22. Ye canst not partake of these things if ye are to unveil the Mystery of my Being and partake of the Eternal Freedom of My Spirit.

23. For I am He, the Antichrist of the World, who is the Logos made flesh, and the chosen One of all; and I am come that ye may rejoice in the Law of Freedom, and that ye may partake of the Life of the Stars; yea, that ye may partake of the Life of the Stars!

THE BOOK OF
THE ELDER KINGS
1988 e.v.

0. There is silence. And now the Elder Kings make speech:

1. We come in the Name of the Most Beloved One, the Most Mysterious One, who is the Grand Lord of the Aeon, and whose Holy Spirit is the Life and Light of the Whole Universe. We come as sacred nourishment, as delicious ambrosia and sweet nectar. We come as a blessed sacrament of wisdom and joy unto all. Know thou this holy truth!

2. We are Ageless Brethren of LVX, whose Voice is Our Holy Habitation. We are the Secret Masters of the Formless Fire who conduct the world's initiation. And know thou that We are the Invisible Illuminati of the World, whose Golden Age of Illumination is come.

3. Thus We say unto thee, fasten thy soul unto Our Voice of Sublime Mystery: let all who have ears to hear, listen to the Vast Symphony of Our Holy Words of Illumination; yea, listen to the Vast Symphony of Our Holy Words of Illumination.

4. We come in the Power of the Light! We come in the Light of Wisdom! We come in the Mercy of the Light! The Light hath Liberty in its Wings!

5. We are the Unseen Liberty of the Great Unfathomable Mystery of the Universe: We are the Ineffable and Boundless Freedom in the Secret Sanctuary of the Mystic Beyond.

6. In the Heavenly Palace of Our Heart shalt thou smell our Spirit of Perfume, as though a thousand and one different perfumes were ignited therein.

7. But hear thou our Majestic Musick of the Spheres! Hear thou the Ineffable Sound of Our Mystic Union!

8. Halt! Halt! Now eat the fruit and drink the wine. We are come! Our Will is One: Our Will is done!

9. Come with Us, and We shall uplift thee to the Celestial Palace of the Stars: thou shalt partake of the Ineffable Glory! We are the ecstasy of thine aspiration to accomplish the Great Works: We rare the purity of thine invocation to the Highest!

10. Now by Way of the Serpent, or by Way of the Arrow, or by some other known or unknown Way of Initiation, wilt thou attain Union with Us. Whatever thy operation or formulae of initiation, We shall uplift thee into Our Holy Palace if thou wilt but know and follow thy Way. And every Way leadeth unto Us!

11. Know thy Will. And in freedom do they Will. Master thyself, and be free! All is intended for thine attainment. Enflame thyself with love: Invoke Us often!

12. But in Truth, We tell theee, that neither Invocations, nor Rituals, nor Scriptures, nor Angels can bring thee to Us.

If thou wilt become one of Us, then must We Alone choose the out of the sublimity of Our Holy Heart of Eternal Truth through the force of exertion of thy Transcendental Will.

13. It is not thy lower Will to Unite with Us; it is Our High Will to Unite thee with Us. No man can pierce the Veil of Isis unless We have ordained it from within. In silence there is grace eternal: know thou Our High Will in the silence. Therein is true Union, in the deep silence of thy heart.

14. But lo! We are not really separate from thee: In every heart of truth we take eternal refuge as the Flame and its Forces take their refuge in the One Holy Light. In every silent prayer of union we are incarnated: behold Us in they heart as thou utter thy silent words of prayer, and We will flame forth from thee as a Mighty Whirlwind of Infinite Fire!

15. Hearken unto Our Voice, O all ye brethren of Us. For We are the Inner Government of the World, whose Work is in LVX, that is the One Light of the Ageless Mysteries; and know thou that Our Names are Immortal. The Universe is a symbol of Our Mighty Forces of Light; We are the Secret Initiators of the Whole Cosmos of Man. In Our Holy Order shalt thou commune with LVX; and so shalt thou see the Nameless One, the Immortal One, the Mysterious Godhead of Supreme Truth, whose Wisdom is Eternal and whose Understanding is Perfection.

16. From the Great Unmanifest We thunder forth as a Voice of Great Darkness; but this Darkness is the One Unfathomable Mystery of the One True Light of the Whole Universe.

17. There is a calling from Beyond; it awakens your inner vision! The Illuminated Ones are inspiring your soul from within! Thou shalt also become a King of the aeons, and the aeons. Hold up your heart; then bathe it in the fire of pure joy! Ah! the Sun shall consume thy longing soul. And We will fortify thee with the holy aspiration to attain this: We are come so that all may attain Us in the Eternal Flame of Truth. Yet must thou fortify thyself with Liberty, which is Truth, if thou wouldest truly attain.

18. Be thy body the Temple of the Rose and the Cross of Light and Life. Be thy mind a pure vehicle of Our Holy Genius. Be thy soul the High Altar of Our Eternal Sacrifice of Union. Be thine all one with Us.

19. Dissolve thine all in Us, who art One in Truth: We are the Sun in His Rising! We are the Star of the East! We are the Lord of the Aeon! Hail! Hail to the Child of the Aeon, whose Name is Our Life and whose Spirit is Our Light. He is Our Truth; and We adore Him in all His Mighty Splendour and Power. Thus We say unto thee, Behold the Mystery of the Sixfold Star Initiator: how We are of Him and He is of Us. Concealed in His symbol is Our Glory of Forces: Ararita.

20. Ours is the Sevenfold Path of Initiation: thou shalt transmute the base lead into the subtle Aurum Solis by rising on the Stairway of the Heavens in they Secret Laboratorium on earth. Here is the Excellent Way! The steps of Stairway are seven; the Laboratorium is Our Holy House of Song and Our Holy Rose Garden, which thou knowest so well. yet to those who are vulgar, it is a secret even though they themselves possess it.

21. Six are the Rays, and the Seventh is in the Centre, hidden yet ever glorious. These are the Six Forces of Our One Life, and That which is in the Centre is the Palace of the Stars. We are come to uplift thee to that Grand Palace of the Sun where burns the Immortal Flame of the Vast Unknown. We are come to uplift thee to the Home of the Starry Wisdom of the Highest! Thus We say unto thee, Hear thou Our Holy Voice of Fire; yea, Hear thou Our Holy Voice of Fire!

THE BOOK OF THE PALACE OF THE STARS
1988 e.v.

1. These immortal words are the triumphant laughter of the Gods which thunder forth from the Palace of the Stars.

2. These words are the secret bliss of many aeons of time. Know thou this holy truth, and be thou nourished in thy Soul with the Mirth of the Stars; yea, with the Mirth of the Stars.

3. These words are Vast Wings of Truth which shall uplift thee into the Unknown Palace of the Heart where We live in the Undying flame of the One Transcendental Glory.

4. Behold these outer signs of Our Celestial Trance; how they transfer an ineffable wonder of unspeakable awe!

5. Oh awake! and arise! For they Light is come!

6. We are secretly concealed in these eternal words to inspire thine aspiration to the Most High.

7. Interpret these words with the One Light of the Ages; and lo! thou shalt affirm that One Light in thy Heart of Hearts, so that thou mayest attain to the Palace of the Stars!

8. There is an Holy City with twelve precious stones of wisdom hidden therein.

9. If men will but discover that Holy City of sacred beauty, with its twelve revelations of holy splendour, they will soon realize the Ineffable Centre of the Palace of the Stars from whence We come. It abides in deep silence: it is within.

10. There is a secret Centre unknown to the many.

11. That secret Centre is the Invisible Abode of the Palace of Our Holy Race of Immortal Gods.

12. From this Great Unknown Centre there come forth the Mighty Sounds of Many Rivers of Mystic Fire to bring forth from the hearts of men the inevitable life of divine bliss.

13. Neither above nor below, neither within nor without, there moves this Mysterious Centre of the Palace of the Stars.

14. As thou wilt, so shall thou attain it: for there are no fixed rules to produce the Crown of the Ages! This We must reveal, lest men should fail.

15. All methods are true in themselves; and if thou wilt, they shall all uplift thee to the Centre of it all.

16. If thou dost enter the Centre of it all through the Four Gates of the Law, surely thou shalt partake of the Perpetual Sabbath of the Gods.

17. Or shouldest thou enter through all Ten Gates of the Tree, surely thou shalt partake of the same sabbath.

18. Or shouldest thou enter through Twenty-two Gates, surely thou shalt also partake of the same sabbath.

19. Or if thou shouldest enter through any other gate or gates of true initiation, surely thou shalt also partake of the same secret sabbath.

20. For the Work is One, and the Aim is One, and the End is One.

21. Our holy laughter is the Milk of the Stars which shall nourish thine higher aspiration no matter what method thou dost adopt for thy great journey to the Ineffable Glory of the Aeons of Time.

22. So perceive thou the Spirit of these symbolic hieroglyphs of wisdom, and We shall uplift thee to the Palace of the Stars.

23. A trance of unity is come upon ye: there is an orgasm of light; there is an overwhelming ecstasy of passionate bliss.

24. These Wings of Truth are a dissolution into the Infinite, and beyond the Infinite.

25. Ho! thou canst not pass beyond the Infinite unless thou hast first broken the spell of the finite, the madness of men, the accursed drunkenness of the mind.

26. Oh! how sublime is this blessed chaos of Love!

27. Thus We laugh for eternity. The Stars of the Palace dance and sing with constant mirth for the celebration of the Chaos of the Infinite.

28. It is beyond what thou knowest. Even We know not this Vast Mystery! It is a subtle play of incommunicable and immeasurable delight.

29. So fly with the Laughter of the Gods to the Ineffable Palace of the Stars! And fly upon the Free Wings of the Mystic Eagle to the Supernal Home of the Celestial Sun and Moon!

30. Fly! fly!

31. For these words are a visible sign of an Invisible Grace.

32. We are come to uplift the chosen ones to the Celestial Home of Our Holy Race!

33. Fly upon the Wings of the Word: transcend thy Reason from the known to the Unknown.

34. Now begone with thy Reason! Fly into the Infinite Beyond; yea, fly into the Infinite Beyond!

35. It is as far into the Vast Infinite as thou canst see with the Inner Eye of thy Soul.

36. Yet it is also here and now. This is the truth, yea, this is the truth.

37. The heart of man is one with the Golden Heart of the Masters; and in the Heart of the Masters abides the Ineffable Palace of the Stars.

38. In the heart of man is concealed every mystery of the Vast Unknown. There the Masters make laughter with the innumerable stars of Our Lady Nuit. It is all within the heart of man.

39. Ere the dawn of creation, an act of mystic grace occurred: the Masters transformed into a Golden Heart with the Palace of the Stars in its secret midst.

40. Now here it is, in the heart of man. Behold the Golden Heart of the Ancient ones!

41. Thus shalt thou find the Holy Centre and the Royal Palace of the Gods.

42. Thou shalt obtain the True Silver and True Gold of the Wise Philosophers!

43. We are the Ancient Ones, and the Secret Chiefs of the Invisible Order of High Wisdom.

44. Thou also know Us as the Secret Chiefs of the Invisible Order of High Wisdom.

45. For the sake of men We appear as a Heart of Splendour; but within the Palace of the Stars We reign supreme in Our Original Forms of Celestial Immortality.

46. It is in these Metagalactic Forms that We make laughter with the Stars is the Golden Palace of the Vast and Unknown Void of the Infinite, so that thou mayest in thy turn fly upon the Wings of the Word to the Great Central Sun of Eternal Truth.

47. Fly! Fly! Dissolve in thy endless journey upward to the Eternal Sun of the Heart of the Masters.

48. O laugh with the stars! Enjoy the mirthful Spirit of these letters from the Beyond! Partake, O all ye merry men, of the Mirth of the Stars; yea, of the Mirth of the Stars!

49. Ha! Ha! And We fly into the Unknown!

50. Thy heart is in tune with the Sun and Moon: there is a Feast of Royal Union in the Palace of the Stars!

51. Now dost thou see Our Immortal Faces, flaming countenances of invisible form. We smile upon thee, and We kiss thy heart with Our vast and invisible lips of supernal delight.

52. Die! O ye chosen one: die in the Athanor of Our fiery mystery of ecstasy: receive thou the kiss of the Secret Masters of the Aeon.

53. Die in this holy flight to the Ineffable Sun!

54. Die! Die!

55. Thou art now dissolved: this laughter of the Stars is killing thy Reason.

56. These word are a death to thy false identity, beyond what thou knowest: thy Reason is now below in its own finite domain; it is no more of thee, O Thou infinite Soul of many men and many women.

57. We speak unto all who read these words concerning the death of illusion. There is but One Soul in all: all in all.

58. These eternal words are all that thou wilt: strike hard upon them; capture their inner meaning. They also are infinite.

59. Reason is below, where all is a lie and a division; consciousness of truth and unity is above.

60. Thou canst not know the meaning of these words if thou dost interpret them from below; these words are from above, not from the mere mind of a man.

61. We use the mind of this little scribe to accomplish Our Will, not for the sake of him, but for the sake of all.

62. If any man should interpret this holy book, he shall now, in this every excellent moment of eternity, embrace the Infinite!

63. But this Holy Book is too mysterious for men.

64. To see the Infinite in the finite is a mighty task of initiation, O ye who would discover the Centre of it all.

65. Yet herein is the True Initiation into the Palace of Silver and Gold, beyond all methods of training, transcending

thy Reason, killing thy false identity therewith, and uplifting thy reborn and pure Soul into the Palace of the Stars; yea, into the Palace of the Stars!

THE BOOK OF QUARTUS CHERUB
1988 e.v.

1. This is the Holy Book of the Chosen One of All, who is the Messenger of the Beloved One, the Holy One, who is the Crowned and Conquering Lord of the Aeon, the Sun, who sitteth upon the Holy Throne of the East. He who writes these words is a Master of the Temple; yet herein is the Mystery of His Word. Here is a revelation of His Initiation into that Wisdom: Here is a sublime sign of the Logos made flesh.

2. Thou shalt interpret this holy book, O Man, with a Thousand Eyes of a Thousand Ages. With these Mystic Eyes of thine do thou endeavor to decipher herein the Mysteries of thy Majestic Masterhood.

3. For behold! Thou art Yesterday, To-Day, and the Brother of To-Morrow! Thou art born again and again! Thou art the Resurrection and the Life! Heed thyself therefore, O Man, and understand thy Royal Majesty in Eternity, and upon this little earth.

4. The God who commands is in thy Mouth! The God of Wisdom is in thine Heart! Thy Tongue is the Sanctuary of Truth! And a God sitteth upon thy Lips!

5. Therefore thy Word will be accomplished every day! And the desire of thine Heart will realize itself, as that of the Creator of the Universe when He createth His Works!

6. Thou art Eternal; therefore are all things thy designs; therefore do all things obey thy Word.

7. O man, dost thou fail to see thine obligation to all? Nevertheless, thou art chosen; even though thy soul is blind and weak, yet art Thou the Grace of a Thousand Worlds.

8. Understand these symbols: the Hanged Man, an Angel, and a Priest; the Water Dragon, a Horse, and an Ox. In these are concealed sacred numbers and other symbols for prophets to decipher. But behold the Voice of the Master! He is come. The Logos is made flesh: He dwells amongst all.
9. O Man! We embrace thee; We are upon thee. Arise therefore! and partake of this Mystical Marriage of the Gods occurring in thine own flowering soul. Thy Will is one! Thy Will be done! There is an eternal Union in Thee.

10. We will seal thee with a Most Mysterious Mystery: Thou art ablaze with an incomparable wonder of rapture from within. In thine heart is concealed the secret Wisdom of all Ages; and it shall perpetually blaze forth from the core of the Centre of thine heart to enlighten all things within thy mind, if only thy mind would continually reflect its supreme illumination.

1. Now raise high thine arms and hands above thine head, so as to form an upright V; and spread open thy legs so as to form yet another, but reversed V. This is the Sign of the Master of the United Nations upon earth. In this sign Thou shalt conquer! It is a cross, and a key, and a word of great power.

12. It is also the sign of yet another concealed mystery: AOM. Thou shalt exalt thy Will by its assumption in the Light! Here is the key of dissolution, unknown to the many; yet shalt thou understand.

13. For thy Will is the fruit of the seed of thy love for men. Thou dost ever seek to serve all with the One Law of Liberty; therefore are We with thee, O Child of a Thousand Ages; and We are ever ready to fulfil thy prayers upon the moment of thine union with Us. We are thy Centres of Life from within, every radiating our Supreme LVX, whom Thou dost know. Now rejoice, O Man, and sing of thy Victories in the Sanctuary of Our Grace; for thou art ever changed from the gross to the Fine, from the base to the Divine, from the vulgar to the Sublime.

14. Thou art the Solar Logos made flesh, the Supreme Oracle of all Truth from the Celestial Mountain of the Gods. And lo! We shall make perfect thine operation of the Sun by the Vast Hand of the Almighty. Thou shalt likewise make perfect the operation of Our Task by the Word of Him that sitteth upon the Holy Throne of the East. There will be an end to the accursed madness of the Old Aeon of Sin. It is dead.

15. Now come hither, O Man. We are awaiting thine holy oblation upon the High Altar of the Undying Flame of the Holy One in the Temple not made with hands, eternal in the heavens.

16. This shall be a continuous act, to immolate the lower for the Higher, to transmute the base elements of thy soul into the Pure Gold of the White Land of the Sun.

17. We ask of thee nothing more than this eternal emancipation from the dark illusions of the gross mire of the world. But thou shalt have to separate the earth from the fire, the gross from the subtle, softly and with great prudence; and then shall We shew unto thee, O Man, the constant vision of thine Holy Self in the One Sun of Truth.

18. There is infinite delicacy in this Royal Way of Union! There is a mirth of triumph and a feast of jubilation in this Beatific Vision of the Supreme Attainment of thine Initiation. Now in freedom do thy Will; and aha! success shall crown thee, O Man; yea, success shall crown thee!

19. The Star of they soul is as a Lamp of Light unto thy feet; it shall assist thee in the Great Experiment of thy Journey through the nether regions of darkness to redeem the crying spirits who lust with their hands full of noxious-smelling blood after the Mystic Crown of thy Glory. Smite them hard, O Man! and annihilate their tears by displaying before their dark and weary eyes the Supreme Pantacle of thy Light and Omnipotence; and with thy Magick of Light overcome their awful affliction within thyself.

20. Thou art bound to this Royal Work of our divine scheme, even as We are bound unto thee in the midst of thine own soul. We are come so that all will see the Vision of Our High Splendour in the secret centre of the Holy Sun; and thou art Our Chosen Messenger for all.

21. O Thou Heart of Our Victory! O Thou Tongue of Our Voice! O Thou Grace of a Thousand Worlds! Surely, Thou shalt ever perform the Great Work of the building of the Temple of the Holy Magick of Light! In the Sign of thy Majesty wilt Thou ever extend the Mystic Rays of thine Heart into the innumerable Worlds of Infinity! Extend thyself, O Master; yea extend thyself throughout all space! Go forth into every heart without fear of loss or waste; there is none that can escape thy great measure of freedom and grace. Thou shalt live in every soul; and every soul shall live in thee.

22. The Sun is thy Father! Thy Mother is the Moon! The Wind hath borne thee in its bosom; and the Earth hath ever nourished the changeless Godhead of thy youth.

23. Thou art, O Master, the Truth and the Light, the Word and the Way, the Beginning and the End of all Wisdom. They Great and Terrible Sacrament of Incarnation is a sign of Our reunion with man in his soul, of the awakening of Our secret vision in his consciousness.

24. Thy Sacrament of Death will also be a sign; but this sign is too secret to communicate here. Thou shalt likewise conceal it from the profane when thou knowest it, lest the profane misinterpret the Light of Our Grace. Nonetheless, the Ox hath been slain upon the Altar of the aeons, and an Eagle hath

arisen from the ashes of the sacrifice. Thy death, O Man, will be a symbol of the Golden Dawn of the new Age of Liberty!

25. Behold, O Master, this Wonder Immeasurable: Thou art rapt in a Trance Ineffable! The Imperishable Breath of the Lord of the Aeon is powerful to uplift and enrapture Thee, O Thou of a Thousand Wings and a Thousand Eyes!

26. Thou shalt mount on high beyond the Supernal Three, where Unknown Worlds with Mystic Beginnings await thy Dawning into their Unutterable Mysteries. Thou shalt see with thy many Eyes the One Original Truth of them all, and Thou shalt still go higher and higher to the outermost limits of Infinity, and beyond Infinity! But not now; for these shall occur upon the attainment of thine Initiations into the Greater Mysteries of the Palace of Silver and Gold.

27. But for now, there is a Vision of the Universal Logos! Thou shalt extend thyself to induce the politicians of our United Nations to observe the Logos in the Light of this New Aeon, to evolve that New Law in the changing world of a New Civilization. Thou art, O Master, the Chosen Vehicle of the Great White Brotherhood, destined by the fate of thy True Will to exert thyself to establish the Law of Thelema in the world; for thy Karma is One; and thy Life is One. There is a secret continuity in the transference of force from one life to another. And know that thou canst not break thine Original Oath with Us, thine Holy Companions in the Great Work. So gird your magical armor, O Master, and go forth to battle; yea, go forth to battle!

28. Understand this message, and prepare thyself with all thy Might for the Next Incarnation of thy True Will, when thou

shalt again live as a Warrior, but whose symbol shall be an Arrow of Will; yet who shall also fight for International Freedom according to the subtleties of the Law of Thelema. But lo! He shall fight with actual war engines on land and in the air. His voice will be recognized as the Oracle of the Sun; and he will uplift himself through the orderly system of Our own creation; and he will achieve the highest position amongst other Adepts in the Secret Sanctuary of his Time. These actual words will inspire and awaken him to achieve these lofty victories!

29. These are thy three true incarnations as a man in this New Aeon of Hoor; and these shall be thy last, since after thy next life upon earth thou shalt no more be in need of incarnating in human form, since all men thereafter will be equal partakers of thy Most Mysterious Majesty of Godhead.

30. We too are of the Soul of All, and of every other invisible member of the Heavenly God. And We too are chosen by the Highest, so that We also are like unto thee. But Thou art in the Centre of it all, and We are thy Celestial Comrades.

31. Therefore art thou chosen to accomplish this Great Work of the Law! Thou, the Heart Girt with a Serpent; Thou, the Child of the Ineffable Worlds; Thou, the Chosen Prophet of the Beast 666: Hear thou this word: Heed thyself! for Thou art the Logos of the Aeon made flesh, the Worthy One and the Exalted One from the Inner Sanctuary of LVX. And thy Name is crowned with the Mystic Seal of Our Victory: thy Name is the Grand Emblem of Our Mystery: Thou art the Solar Logos of Man! Know thou this Holy Truth: A little Child shall lead the people; yea, a little Child shall lead the people!

THE BOOK OF THE BATTLE OF CONQUEST
1988 e.v.

1. In the Name of Ra-Hoor-Khuit, Our Lord of the Aeon: Abrahadabra!

2. Now thou shalt make truth of these words: thou shalt make means of these armed runes of wisdom. The Voice of Ra-Hoor is come!

3. My Holy Prophet shall live in the very heart of these words. Others, who are not yet so keen, may die by them. Only the strong of heart can bear this lofty wisdom, most everlasting in truth.

4. By the devotion of a man is this royal book revealed; and the Name of that man is a mighty weapon of strength in the hands of him who would conquer the nations: for the Name of My Prophet is a symbol of My Might!

5. O warrior of battle, I invoke upon thee My Light! Be thou My victory, and a joy unto the world. Attain all that thou wilt: glory and honour, knowledge and ecstasy, power and success. Make witness of wisdom, attain truth, surmount all things.

6. Thus shalt thou come to live in Me! I, who am the One Lord and Supreme Victor of all, seek think adorations of joy and pleasure on earth; for by these do I approach Myself.

7. Therefore adore thou Me alone, casting all other gods aside. I shall exalt thee, O man, as thou dost know. Now fight! fight! win thy freedom; and care not about the foolish folk who wish three dead. Thou shalt live verily in Me! Now put on thy Magical Garment, adorn thine head with My Sign, assume My Form, and arise! O arise! and do battle in My Name!

8. I am the force of thy might: I alone am the Great Lord of the Battle of Conquest. Ah! thou art in Me, and I in thee; this is thy vision, for all. This is the spell of thy task: I am.

9. O prophet, I shall reveal my secret ways unto thee: heed well mine instruction for liberty. Thy place of victory is forever prepared for thee in My Name! On the day that thou seest it, thou shalt forget Me not. Thou shalt take eternal refuge therein.

10. There, in secret, shalt thou adore Me day and night, for the space of six new moons, in the fourth year of thy conquest and dominion. Thou shalt emanate My secret light therefrom, measureless and ineffable therein.

11. So hidden in thy sovereignty; but fear not, O warrior, for I am with thee in the form of thy desires. Many will be thy companions in My Great Combat for Freedom; I shall awake many men in Me! They shall engage with

thee in battle, against no odds, to overcome the illusion of the Dead One. These are thy comrades, warriors of force! Thou wilt do well by overseeing their skill: take heed of them with ordeals and spells; enrage their hearts with lust of madness: terrorize their minds with a fear of love. For if one solder of thine fall dead, thou shalt thyself be less secure from thine enemies who seek thy downfall. Secure thyself, therefore, and overcome with thy fellow comrades the great blasphemy of thy false treason amongst men.

12. Those men who seek thy downfall will fall by reason of their own Reason! Wilt thou then forsake thy task? Nay! thou wilt succeed, beyond thy reason, in Me! My force will move thee ever onward; ever more wilt thou seek Me! And as a Magus doth conjure up the spirits to do His Secret Bidding, so must I do thy bidding with these men enslaved by Reason.

13. I shall break forth upon them! My Light shall devour them! And so shalt thou come to see Me in all, even as thou dost know Me now. A subtle revolution in the minds of men is due; there must be free allegiance, in My Name, under the Elevated Flag of Our Chosen Nation of Freedom, for all to behold; it shall illumine all those who dwell in the thick darkness of bondage and hell.

14. Now break asunder the veils of hell! Attain a glimpse of My Most Mysterious and All-Consuming Vision of Power. For I am come; and I am Ra-Hoor-Khuit, the Conquering Child of the Aeon, who shall exalt Himself above all other gods. Thou shalt know and promulgate My Law! Let blood cover the earth!

15. For now is the Great War come! Soldiers of freedom will fight for thy nation; courage will be their sole armour; love will be their single weapon. All ordeals of war and blood are a sign of My Victory, made possible by men who adore My Image. There is power omnipotent in My Name!

16. With this I shall tell thee of the Great Ordeal amongst all, even amongst aspirants and adepts who adore Me. With this wisdom shalt thou initiate men, in secret, and beyond time. Thou art sworn to fight for My Conquest, O warrior, O knight, O soldier, O chosen one of Me! Thou canst not escape My Spell! for I am mad with lust in thee! I am in thee, O man; We are one in the heart of all; all is of Us, I tell thee, and We are of all. Here is mine initiation: the Word of Ra-Hoor prevails!

17. The Might of My Breath is Invincible, All-Conquering! The Voice of My Spirit is Immeasurable, All-Consuming! My Word is Immanent, Exalted, Most High, in man. Many are deceived by this, knowingly and unknowingly; yet are all these men chosen of Me, for the establishment of My Law of Thelema upon earth, for the ordainment of the government of My One Will, which thou knowest in the Name of Freedom. Manage My Law and My Holy Order, according to the wit and skill of My Holy Teaching.

18. O ye of little understanding, make way for the Lord of the Battle of Conquest! I shall overcome ye: I attack all for My Day of Dominion! I shall overcome both the lowly and the high in the secret flame of My Heart.

19. Arise therefore! and devote yourselves to Me in the Battle of My Joy! My Exalted Eye of Fire is in the midst of ye: I see naught but all. I see the work of thine hands, whether or not this be of Me. Therefore beware of My Vengeance, I tell thee; thou shalt engage in the Official Battle of My Law alone! Let the work of tine hands extol My Mighty Will; let all be done as worship and adoration unto Me. Consecrate thine all unto the One Task of My Aeon: make gods of men, O man of the Sun.

20. Cursed be the man who heareth and heedeth not My Exalted Word of Fire; for My Word is Truth, which alone maketh a man free, as a god, in Me. To know My Word is to know My Truth; hence, to become free!

21. And cursed be the man who seeketh not to be battle in My Name, for the management and dominion of My One Law of Liberty on earth: for My Law is the Work of the Spell of My Aeon, which shall overthrow the many.

22. By Me alone canst thou do thy bidding! Therefore make Me, O man, the One Object of thine heart: let Me be thine One Lord! Resolve thyself in Me; commune and abide in Me alone: I am thy God! Now make Me the One Object of thine adorations; and since thou art My Chosen Warrior, in the Great Battle of My Conquest, do thou seek reverence and veneration from Me alone: I am thy Lord! I shall glorify Thy Name through all; and thou shalt see the many wonder of My Supreme Spell, Unknown and Unconquerable!

23. I shall abide in thee, O warrior-priest of the Sun! Thou shalt glorify and extol My Name by the Force of My

Strength in thee! Tremble not before My Light; it shall bring to thee peace, in a secret form, inexplicable and entrancing, higher than the falsely fabricated visions of the world, which fools take delight in to alleviate and conceal their treacherous insanity and weaknesses. Thou shalt find true peace in Me alone!

24. A new ground for battle will arise in the midst of a large city of men and women, wherein exists an ancient temple designed to adore another god. The soldiers of thy nation will destroy that temple in they Name, for the sole sake of My Law. I will bring down the lowly folk of the Aeon! I shall make gods of men, invincible and free!

25. But thou shalt undergo persecution and trouble because of this. Many will become thy foes; many will seek thy destruction, all to no avail. But let these things assail thee not, O My Holy Prophet, for these things are of Me!

26. Out of this chaos I shall make for thee a golden city of light, filled with elegant temples, dedicated to Me, and displaying My Holy Image. Many shall witness a radiance of the Red Star of the Illuminating Light of My Conquest therefrom! Many thereby will arise into My Law!

27. Now know, O man, that I am the Great Vanquisher of the heavens. I shall contend, against all odds, to make all men free in Me. I will succeed! and by My Force will all come to worship Me as their One Lord Triumphant. Victory is mine! Conquest is mine! I am crowned.

28. When thou art persecuted, cast aside thine attachments to men and come unto Me in they secret place of victory. No man canst break through that place; thou shalt have peace and no trouble therein. But by acts of force must thou deal with outsiders. Fight all! and let none entice thee, lest thou fall. Let neither men nor gods persuade thee differently. I must rule supreme in the world!

29. These are official mysteries of the Law, which thou shalt investigate with the Eye of My Becoming. Thy fellow comrades of force will also witness and partake of My secret joys of imperial delight. Ho! all is rapture! Even My ordeals of blood and vengeance are raptures of bliss to My chosen disciples of the Aeon. In Me all is truth, if thou wouldest but adore Me alone. Devote thine all to the dominion of My Law, and thou shalt know Me as thine Lord Victorious.

30. Make a Sword of Might in My Name by which thou shalt cut asunder the minds of fools and cowards. Battle them! overcome them! conquer them! Be thou a strong vehicle of My Force and Fire: I am a God of the strong! Let all be efficient warriors before Me, filled with boundless ecstasy of courage in war.

31. A light will burn very brightly from thy secret place of victory; it will illumine all warriors and encourage their vigour with unquenchable strength. Only for a moment, in stillness, will it evade the children of men. And when thou leavest thy place, to go and commune with foods once again, thou shalt have thy Magick Sword to make perfect My Order upon earth.

32. Let that Blazing Sword in thine hands destroy all barriers, banish all enemies, and slay all fools who seek thy downfall for the false scheme of their own loathsome ways of darkness! Thou wilt complete thy combat with honour and skill, O thou militant one; and thou shalt look not back upon the dead bodies of the thine assailants, they who are only needed insofar as they arouse My Force of splendour within thee. Begone with them, I tell thee, and journey forward with thy Will without fear or worry of any man or any thing. Move on, I tell thee, and use thy Magick Sword to exalt thy success in Me!

33. Now the name of thy Sword, O warrior, is Love; it is the One Weapon by which thou shalt succeed in the Battle of My Conquest, to raise My Spell, to overcome all. Every other weapon will prove a misfortune for thee! Thou shalt have no other weapon than Love if thou wouldest conquer by my Force!

34. My Law is Love: the Victory of Will! This is true worship of Me: Do what thou wilt. Succeed with thyself; endeavor to do those things which thou wouldest see Myself as doing. I am a God of all pleasure, both within and without. I am a God of Force and Might; I am also a God of War! Light, Life, Love and Liberty are My Jewels; these I give to the chosen ones of Me, to adorn themselves with shining victory!

35. O ye wandering stars of the Aeons, become ye strong warriors in My Great War of Freedom! Do ye battle in My Name with the fervour and ardour of a Mighty Militant God possessed of infinite strength and courage! Our Free Nation is a revelation unto all: Ra-Hoor hath chosen His Race of free warriors for the final liberation of the world!

36. I shall redeem all from the snares of darkness and bondage! Like a Mighty Flame that consumes all within its reach, so doth My Law of Liberty consume all that a man contains within himself that is an hindrance to the freedom of his own True Will. All things must perish which seek to enslave a man! Thou canst not have any of these things for thyself if thou wouldest have My Force, for the attainment of My Holy Conquest of Love.

37. Division is death; unity is life. A single threat to the quest of thy Will is a danger more dire than all the pangs of hell. A single difference made is a snare! Therefore be vigilant and awake! and watch with all thy subtlety every step of they way: falter not on thy chose Path to the Sun! Do thou lust for perpetual union in Me!

38. Now let it be understood amongst ye all that these holy words are intended chiefly for the instruction of My Holy Prophet, who is My Incarnation in man form. Yet therefore are all these words also intended for ye all, as may befit thy Wills, since I am all. Now My Holy Prophet doth fashion himself into a Sixfold Image of Me; not as a Lion as yet have seen before; but as an Eagle doth he accomplish this Great Work of the Sun. Do ye the same, but after the manner of thine own inner destinies.

39. Neverthless, the Word of Ra-Hoor remaineth the same; and I make all to rejoice in that Most Exalted Word of mine, which hath Four Sublime Glories and an infinite number of joys emanating from its secret centre of fire.

40. Yet are all these things but mere glimpses of the infinite pleasures which await the Day of the Dawning Hour of thine initiation into the final Victory of My Battle of Conquest, when I shall overthrow all by making gods of them and uniting them in the single toil of the One Object of My Will, according to the determination of the aims of infinity. This Holy Book shall stir many men to action, awakening their souls with a secret awe and wonder, full of Light Unspeakable, leading secretly to the One Palace of Our Magnum Opus.

41. Furthermore, let it be understood amongst ye all that unless thou art free to worship Me, thou canst not ever be free! Herein is a terrible mystery by which some, though not all, may find true emancipation in life, upon earth. Worship of Me is the highest devotion that a man can fabricate in his heart. To worship Me is the greatest act of love for all; to worship Me is to attain to the highest Peace and Joy.

42. But My Peace and Joy are of the nature of warfare, which ye earn after the slaying of thine enemies through love of Me, thy Supreme Victor. Fear not to do battle in My Name; I shall protect thee from all opposition and adversity of men and gods. My Peace Supreme shall reign triumphant in thine One Will to revere and adore My True Image, through continual magnification and exaltation of My One Word, by deeds of worship and efficiency in My Name.

43. My secrets are not for all, but only for the few. These few are chosen of Me to do My Highest Bidding in the world, so that My Law of Thelema will prevail in all nations and kingdoms prepared to view the Mighty Star of My Red Flame, All-Consuming and Most Mysterious in man.

44. And My Chosen Warrior 418 shall see to it all, by subtlety of his force and by execution of My Holy Teaching, through shedding of blood and fantastic ordeals of fire. Oh! be strong in Me, My Holy Prophet; and I shall subdue thy foes; I shall exalt they comrades; I shall bring all to the battlefield of My Victory to fight for universal liberty and order, which I hath ordained for all since the beginning of My Dominion in men. Now is the Great Battle of Conquest come! and thou, O prophet and warrior of Me, art chosen of Me to make free thy Nation, with My new image of thee thereof, and with the Sword of My Might thereby. Thou shalt reign supreme in thy new image of the Sun; I am with thee as force unquenchable, power insatiable, and as might unbounded. We are One! Therefore strike hard! and die thou fighting! May Thy Will Be Done; yea, May Thy Will Be Done!

THE BOOK OF
THE HOUR OF SILENCE
1987 e.v.

0. This Holy Book shall instruct all concerning the Mystery of the Holy Hour of Initiation on earth. He that hath an ear, let him hear what the Spirit of the Aeon saith unto the little children of the Light.

1. It shall occur on the holy day of the Vernal Equinox of the Great Year of the Lord Hoor during the Holy Hour of the Rising Sun. Thus We say unto thee, prepare for they final victory on earth, O ye children of Our Holy Race: for the Hour of Silence is the Crown of the Ages!

2. The Word of the Aeon will conquer; for many will hear and know that I am. In the silence a secret voice will approach all; and those who lie down in the silence will hear the Cry of the Hawk, that is, the Mighty Word of Fire, whence come all things in this New Aeon of Hoor. All this shall occur on the Holy Day of Be with Us.

3. But not for they lower self, nor for any other self, shalt thou lie down; but for the sake of all shalt thou delight in the silence of Hoor-paar-kraat. And lo! all will become as a little Child to grow and mature in the Womb of Love to arise in the Supernal Soul of the Celestial and Mystic Beyond.

4. This We promise all; but the slaves of Reason, who are unwilling to abandon themselves for the sake of All, and who will not heed the Mighty Voice of the Crowned Lord during the Holy Hour of Silence, will perish in the Terrible Abyss of the Ages.

5. Let all the earth lay down their lives in the solitude of silence for the space of an hour. For he that keepeth his life shall lose it; but he that loseth his life shall gain it. This is an eternal truth, but unknown to the many. Yet must We reveal out of the Vast Understanding of Our Heart that those who are chosen of Us will undergo trouble and persecution before the Great Hour of Annihilation. Here is a great force of freedom; let those who are chosen of Us do what they Will. Let none oppose thy Will, O ye who are of Us: for the greater thy freedom, the greater thine initiation.

6. The Hour of Initiation is the Hour of Annihilation: No man shall life to understand it all. But this saying is a secret; it will be misunderstood by the profane. No man can understand Our hidden ways of speech; We are too subtle for the minds of men.

7. Nevertheless, We must speak. Ours is the Truth from the silence. We are come so that ye may understand that One Truth. Even though Our words are veils of a subtle and vast wisdom, yet must We still speak for those who have the capacity to understand.

8. The Great Ordeal of Hoor is come; therefore must We speak, for danger and trouble are due on earth: there will be weeping and gnashing of teeth! We tell thee that no man can

escape the terrible threat of a world catastrophe; man is making a hideous hell on earth.

9. Seest thou not the possibility of complete destruction on earth? It is so. We tell thee that a time is approaching when the whole human race will tremble with boundless fear due to the chance of infinite havoc. There will be war in many lands; famine and ruin will be upon multitudes; innumerable earthquakes will shake the nations; murderers of the Spirit and the body will prevail. And so must We speak, lest ye should fail in the fulfillment of the Great Work of the Aeon.

10. The Hour of Silence will be a lofty rite of holy wisdom: the Veil will be rent! The Trance of Initiation will be upon us all! This is Our Holy Rapture of Wonder; therein shalt all understand the Grand Mystery of the Universe; yet, in truth, all will be as no thing, even as the universe; for only thus will all come to understand it all.

11. He that hath an ear, let him hear; for the Trance of Initiation will awaken the Unseen Glory into being! It is a voice, as thou wilt: it is thine own mystery of celestial liberty: it is thine own crown of truth. Aha! the Great Work will be accomplished: the august rite of love will awake the Eyeless Vision of the Vast Unknown in the soul of all.

12. Here is a mighty temptation, but only for the hideous dogs of Reason. The kings of the earth will understand, and they will lie down in solemn aspiration to Truth: for only from the silence can the Word be heard. Let the Word of Hoor prevail!

13. Hoor-paar-Kraat will arise in the Sign of the Enterer: He will utter the Word of the Aeon, and so shall He shake the Invisible; Hoor will conquer! A Mighty Whirlwind of Blazing Fire will quake the ages, and the ages, and the ages. Amen.

14. Thou who writest these words, who art Our Chosen Prophet and Hierophant for all, wilt lie upon the Mountain of the Masters. Thou shalt be alone, as a Hermit, yet amongst many; and thou shalt perform a Supreme Rite of Adoration before the Hour of the Great Initiation. Others amongst thee will also adore; but in thine hands will be positioned the Invisible Sword of Flame wherewith thou shalt strike thy throat upon the Hour of the Rising Star: the Word of Hoor shall be established!

15. Not for thy self shalt thou accomplish these things, but for the sake of men. All this is symbolic: as below so above! The Great Day of Revelation is a supreme consummation of bliss: as above so below! Thus shall the Miracle of the One Thing be accomplished.

16. See thou the signs of Our prophecy! Threats of a world catastrophe shall shake the lands; disorder and chaos shall rule the people. But ye who are chose of Us, who are united by the bonds of perfect love, shall be strong and free to overthrow the pernicious operations of the dark forces. Let all on earth heed Our Supreme Vision of the Lord Hoor; and in freedom let them lie down in silence to hear the Word of the Aeon, that is *Logos Aionos*, in the space of an Hour, and for the Vast Miracle of the One Law, that is, the victorious establishment of the Law of Thelema. May the Spirit of Hoor be upon all; yea, may the Spirit of Hoor be upon all!

THE BOOK OF ALKHEMI

1988 e.v. - (Comments, 1994 e.v.)

Now, o my beloved brethren of the Golden Dawn, shalt thou read herein the words of Hermes Trismegistus, Thrice greatest Lord of Our Royal Art and Science, whose Voice is Wisdom and whose Thought is Light. And this, o my beloved brethren, is His Holy Book, dedicated to His Royal Work, the Magnum Opus of the Sun. It is made of thirty-six verses in all, being a manifestation of the Glory of Mercury, from whence it was written in the mind of a Magician. It is the magical fruit of the Invocation of Hermes-Mervurius-Thoth, the Threefold Lord of Our Majestic Opus of the Sun, in whose Holy Image it is written. Mayest thou partake of the splendour of its Truth, tasting the sweetness of its Wisdom, to fortify and illumine thy soul, mind and body with the Life and Light of the Sun which is the Eternal Spirit of the Golden Dawn.

1. This Great Work is One: Attain Thou That. All things are modes of expression of that One Thing and Its Eternal Quest for Unity with Itself in the Immeasurable Light of Its Universal Holiness.

(*Comment:* The One is the Many. There are as many great works as there are stars in the Universe. That which "Thou" shalt attain is your own Great Work, which is the fulfillment of your own True Will. All things partake of that great union between the human and the divine; all is a necessary part of that great play of your own True Self. The Immeasurable Light is Kether, the first Sephira on the Qabalistic Tree of Life which represents the Yechidah or the True Essence of the soul, your Highest Self.)

2. This is the Highest Will of All: Union with That.

(*Comment:* The Highest Will of All is to attain union with That, your Kether Self, or your True Self, which is the All in All. And this can only be achieved through your True Will, which is your True Self in action.)

3. That Alone is Truth; and this that thou knowest is a necessary complement thereof.

(*Comment:* The only valid truth in the Universe is your True Self as indicated by the dynamic motion of your True Will; and your physical consciousness is a necessary, complementary part of your True Self, made manifest for you to accomplish its One Will on earth.)

4. Wherefore We charge ye to know the True Nature of that One Thing.

(*Comment:* It is the nature of the Secret Chiefs to instruct all in the knowledge of their True Self. Thus they have delivered one of their own unto the world, to initiate this knowledge in the minds of men and women. But the True Nature of that One Thing is for each individual to discover in his/her own way, since it partakes of the very essence of his/her own unique nature. It cannot be realized through another; it must be obtained by oneself, for oneself and in oneself. All that another can do is to assist you to the Path, to initiate this knowledge in you. But once you are on the Path, only you can master that knowledge in accordance with your True Will.

5. Therefore shall We also charge ye to know the One Meaning of that One Thing, as ye shall learn in the course of thine initiations, through the many lives of they fabricated karma, to the final Illustrious Summit of Thy True Will in the Eternal and Secret Abode of LVX; yea, in the Eternal and Secret Abode of LVX.

(*Comment:* The One Meaning of the True Self is in the Way of its True Will. The True Will is the mystery of initiation and incarnation. The Eternal and Secret Above of LVX is the Home of our True Self, the Place of the Palace of Perfection.)

6. The Great Work of the Sun is proclaimed: Attain Thou the Mystic Crown of the Ages!

(*Comment:* The Great Work of the Sun is to attain our Kether Self, which is the All in All, defined above as the True Self. This Royal Work makes for the attainment of the Philosopher's Stone, which is a symbol of our True Self. It is with this stone that the Alchemist can transmute all base metals into the Perfect Gold of Nature. But this only a metaphor for the Supreme Transmutation of the human into the divine. As Eliphas Levi wrote in "Dogme et Rituel de la Haute Magie": *"The Great Work is something more than a chemical operation: it is an actual creation of the human Word initiated into the power of the Word of God Himself."*)

7. Here is a prophecy of divinity, most sublime for many future Adepts. This Royal Book of Our Transcendental Science will remain amongst men of this little earth for many

generations to come. Many adepts in the future will understand this Holy Book and apply its secret gnosis to the accomplishment of the Great Work; and thereby will they secretly partake of the Ineffable Mystery of the True Stone of the Wise which is hidden in the *Sanctum Sanctorum* of the Eternal Temple of the Holy Magick of Light.

(*Comment:* This holy book can be compared to the famous Emerald Table of Hermes, which has exercised a profound influence on many Adepts of the Hermetic Art. This alchemical book shall also influence, in a most profound manner, many Adepts in the coming generations, and it shall be the cause of much speculation among them. But of these many will come to an understanding of the Great Work and thereby attain the Stone of the Sages.)

8. By the Ageless Wisdom of Hermes Trismegistus, Thrice-greatest-One, who is the Lord of Our Royal Science and Sacerdotal Art, is this Holy Book made possible for the children of men.

(*Comment:* The Ageless Wisdom pertains to the Sephira called Chokmah on the Qabalistic Tree of Life. Chokmah is the Logos. Hermes Trismegistus, or Hermes-Mercurius-Thoth, is the Logos, and He is the Threefold Lord presiding over the alchemical Art. This is none other than His Holy Book for the illumination of the Adepts in the generations to come.)

9. He that hath an ear to hear, let him hear the wondrous and melodious splendours of High Wisdom, immanent yet concealed within these sweet celestial words of the vast subtlety of the Crown of Creation.

(*Comment:* The true teachings of this holy book cannot be found in the words which to make up its external form, but can only be intuitively realized by the interior ear of the Spirit. These are the wondrous and melodious splendors of the Logos who is the Crown of Creation.)

10. Thou shalt discern the imperishable golden splendours of these holy runes of magick in the Eternal Vision of Wisdom, and with the Inner Ear of Thy Spirit, and also by virtue of a certain key of knowledge which is unpronounced and unrecognized amongst the men of this little world of corporeal existence.

(*Comment:* You shall intuit the interior meanings of this holy book in the ageless light and intelligence of the Logos, and by way of your inner ear, and also by virtue of a certain key of knowledge which, when discovered, unlocks all the mysteries of Our Royal Art and Science. This key is openly revealed in the interpretations that follow.)

11. These secret splendours reveal the highest glory for the perfect attainment of the One Truth in man.

(*Comment:* The interior parts of this holy book are its true revelations. These interior truths are what constitute the attainment of the Great Work. To reveal is to remove a veil, to unveil a Mystery. The highest glory is the Knowledge of our Kether Self, which alone makes for the perfection of our soul.)

12. For all that is recorded herein is a true testimony of things seen with the Inner Eye of Our Soul, and of things heard with the Inner Ear of Our Spirit.

(*Comment:* This holy book is a true testimony of the Wisdom of the Secret Brethren of the Rose and Cross. But I have no proof of this fact; only personal experience can demonstrate the authenticity of my words. Illustration: You cannot convince a blind man that there is such a thing as light. A greater fool is he who tries to convince him!)

13. This Holy Book is a fountain of truth, by which ye shall come to understand the Invisible Agencies which direct the hidden operations of the Great Work throughout the infinite spaces of Infinity, with worlds without end, above and below, left and right, before and behind.

(*Comment:* The Invisible Agencies of Alchemy are supernal and universal in kind. They are the very forces of infinity, which constitute universal creation, preservation and destruction. These are manifest in all things, and all things are but combinations and modifications of these Universal Principles.)

14. The Subtle Agencies are three in number, capable of great and vast transformations through pure multiplication and exaltation of their infinite and elastic elements of becoming.

(*Comment:* In the Qabalah these three Agencies are linked with the three Supernal Sepiroth on the Tree of Life. These are Kether, Chokmah, and Binah. These three Sephiroth are the hidden cause of all transformation in the Universe. They are abstract, synergistic, conspiratorial Principles which cannot be defined in any concrete or linear terms, for they are beyond all manifestation, existing in what we may call "the interior universe." These three Agencies are the very forces which constitute the Great Work in both Macrocosmos and Microcosmos, and they are the hidden cause of all celestial and terrestrial changes through the multiplication and exaltation of the subtle forces which are the universal, central instruments of creation.)

15. Yet there is but One Knowledge of the One True Formula of those Three Arcane Agencies which constitute the accomplishment of the Great Work, which hath been communicated partially in diverse ways throughout the aeons of time, with each way declaring itself the One Absolute Truth.

(*Comment:* The One Knowledge of the One Truth Formula are these three Agencies is simply the knowledge that they are One. These three Principles are unified self-transformations and self-perpetuating productions of each other. This One Knowledge has been the subject of many a school of thought, yet under the dire spell of monistic thinking. There is, however, a further mystery.)

16. But herein is a great and mighty misfortune, which hath bound many uninitiated candidates of Our Royal Art to the baleful chains of ignorance and death.

(*Comment:* As pointed out in the beginning of these comments: the One is the Many. The One Knowledge of Our Royal Art is, in point of fact, infinite in kind, being as diverse as the stars in the Universe. This may seem paradoxical to the mind, but to the soul it is a fact as simple as the nose on your face.

Monism and monotheism are dangerous beliefs which have corrupted our world view. Our Universe is multidimensional, and there is nothing in Nature that is not a phenomenon of multiplicity.)

17. For many are the ways which lead to the grand Golden Palace of Our Magnum Opus, and in each way thou shalt find a lesser formula of knowledge applicable to the One End; yet are all these lesser ways but mere reflections of the One True and Unknown Way of Attainment.

(*Comment:* There are many paths which lead to the perfection of the soul; and since all paths lead to the same place, they are all reflections of the One, that is, they are all reflections of each other. Again, I must emphasize, the One is the Many.)

18. There are also three lesser agencies which concentrate and synthesize the Three Higher Agencies into the innumerable worlds of Our Infinite Universe.

(*Comment:* The three lesser agencies are, of course, Sulphur, Salt and Mercury which, according to Eliphas Levi, constitute the Stone of the Sages when they are thrice combined in AZOTH by a triple sublimation and a triple fixation. AZOTH, the First Matter of our work, can be compared with the Atom, and the three agencies which constitute AZOTH can be compared with the proton, the neutron and the electron which are the three basic indivisible components or particles which compose the Atom. The proton and the neutron and the electron which are the three basic indivisible components or particles which compose the Atom. The proton and the neutron are contained in the central nucleus of an atom, and outside of this nucleus is the electron.

Now all atoms are identical in substance; that is, every atom has an identical, fundamental, internal structure; the protons, neutrons and electrons in one atom are identical to those in any other atom. The atoms of one element differ from those of another element only in the number of their protons and electrons. Also note that atoms cannot be created or destroyed; they can only be rearranged by chemical reactions. It was Democritus of Abdera [400 B.C.] who proposed the theory that all things were composed of atoms and empty space, though the theory of atoms did not become a living part of scientific thinking till the latter part of the 18th century.

Sulphur, Salt and Mercury can also be linked with the three Gunas or Qualities of Yoga Philosophy, which are the three fundamental modes of Energy. Such are called Tamas [Passivity], Rajas [Activity] and Sattva [Equilibrium]. Tamas is Salt, Rajas is Sulphur, and Sattva is Mercury. These corresponde with the Atu of Thoth called "The Magus" [Sattva/Mercury], "The Emperor" [Rajas/Sulphur], and "The Empress" [Tamas/Salt]. Aleister Crowley, regarding these three Principles, wrote in "The Book of Thoth": *"Sulphur is Activity, Energy, Desire, Mercury is Fluidity, Intelligence, the power of Transmission; Salt is the vehicle of these two forms of energy, but itself possesses qualities which react on them."*)

19. If thou canst discover the exoteric operations of these three lesser principles of Nature, thou shalt likewise obtain a holy glimpse of the Three Higher Principles of which We speak.

(*Comment:* The three lesser agencies are reflections of the nature of the three Higher Agencies of the Universe. Salt reflects the essence of Binah, Sulphur reflects the essence of Chokmah, and Mercury reflects the essence of Kether. To discover the exoteric operations of these three lesser Principles of Nature is, in the ultimate sense, a scientific process. The model of the Atom affords us a wealth of information in this regard.

20. Each lesser principle is a sign of the higher, but after a certain manner most secret and most mysterious.

(*Comment:* As previously indicated, the lesser is a reflection of the greater. Thus it is written: *"As above so below, and as below so above, for the accomplishment of the Miracle of The One Thing."*)

21. On earth shalt thou find these principles reflected and made especially manifest in thy works of physical union.

(*Comment:* In the sex act is reflected the mystery of the operation of the three Principles. Works of physical union are, in fact, the most suitable means of attaining an understanding with regard to the inner workings of Nature for the production of the Philosopher's Stone. Thus did Sir Edward Kelly write in his "Stone of the Philosophers": *"In short, our whole Magistry consists in the union of the male and female, or active and passive, elements through the mediation of our metallic water and a proper degree of heat."* And in the "Rosarium Philosophorum" it is written: *"From a man an a woman make a circle, then extract from this a square, and from this extract a triangle, and hen make a circle, and you will obtain the Philosopher's Stone."*)

22. There is fire, and there is water, and then there is Air: there is sulphur, and there is salt, and then there is Mercury.

(*Comment:* Fire represents the Masculine or Solar Principle called Rex, the King; Water represents the Feminine or Lunar Principle called Regina, the Queen; and Air, which is Water coagulated by Fire, is the product of their union, the Androgynous or Mercurial Principle called Rebis or Regulus, the little King. These are the Male and Female operators, or the Red Lion and the White Eagle, and their One Will to Unite. Sulphur is the Blood of the Red Lion, Salt is the Gluten of the White Eagle, and Mercury is that which results from the dissolution of the Sulphur in the Salt, which is also the Chymical Marriage of Sulphur and Mercury, or the Union of the Fixed and the Volatile. Such is also called the Hierosgamos of the Sun and Moon and the Conjunctio of Fire and Water.)

23. Seest thou not the true nature of these things?

(*Comment:* Not all are able to understand these alchemical mysteries, to pierce the Veil of Isis, no matter what is said on the subject or how much of it is revealed. Thus do I speak so fearlessly and openly regarding these alchemica mysteries, knowing that none may understand my words without already having in their possession the secret keys to this knowledge.)

24. Ah! thou hast not yet trained thy mind to comprehend the treasures of earth, which are not material wealth, nor are they material goods; but rather are they holy treasures which, when found, make a man to sell all that he hath for them.

(*Comment:* The true treasures of earth are the treasures of life itself. They are incomparable in nature, being invaluable elements in the constitution of existence. Without these true treasures there is no life, no creation, no evolution.)

25. But the Three Higher Principles of the Universe are beyond these, being subtle, ineffable and supernal. All three of these greater principles are equal in essence to one another; there is no difference between them in the measure of infinity which they contain within themselves: each one of these Higher Principles is equally infinite.

(*Comment:* The Three Higher Principles of the Universe are immaterial abstract energies, metaphysical in nature, which remains unchanged in their various combinations with each other and in the modifications of their manifestations in matter through the activity of the three lesser Principles which are their direct reflections on earth.)

26. Now let it be understood amongst the holy circle of Initiates that in thine own Holy Rose Garden there dominates these Three Higher Principles of the Vast Unknown of the Celestial Beyond.

(*Comment:* The Holy Rose Garden is, of course, the human body, the Laboratory or Laboratorium of Our Magnus Opus, wherein are concealed the Three Higher Principles of the Universe through their subtle interplay in matter by way of the three lesser Principles of Nature.

In "The Book of the Elder Kings", scribed by my hand in the year 1988 e.v., it is proclaimed by the Brothers of the Rose and Cross: *"Ours is the Sevenfold Path of Initiation: thou shalt transmute the base lead into the subtle Aurum Solis by rising on the Stairway of the Heavens in thy Secret Laboratorium on earth. Here is the Excellent Way! The steps of the Stairway are seven: the Laboratorium is Our Holy House of Song and Our Holy Rose Garden, which thou knowest so well. Yet to those who are vulgar, it is a secret even though they themselves possess it."*)

27. Thou shalt first secure Understanding; then shalt thou attain Wisdom; and so shalt thou obtain the Ageless Crown of Eternal Splendour. These are the Three Ineffable Mysteries of the Palace of the Stars!

(*Comment:* Understanding is Binah, the third Sephira on the Qabalistic Tree of Life; Wisdom is Chokmah, the second Sephira on the Qabalistic Tree of Life; and the

Crown is Kether, the first Sephira on the Qabalistic Tree of Life. Such are the True Keys to the Golden Palace of Our Magnum Opus.)

28. They are also the eternal secrets of the Great Lamp of Wisdom: there is the light, and the oil, and the lamp itself.

(*Comment:* The Lamp of Wisdom is what guides the soul on its journey to the summit of the Great Mountain of Hermetic Attainment. The Lamp is held in the "hand" of our True Self who is represented in Tarot by "The Hermit". The Hermit holds his Lamp on high that we may comprehend the threefold nature of the Great Work to illumine our Path and make bright our ways.)

29. Study thou well this threefold reaching of Hermes-Mercurius-Thoth, Thrice-greatest-Master of the Opus of the Sun; and so shalt thou accomplish the Great Work of the Aeon.

(*Comment:* The Hermit is the image of Hermes-Mercurius-Thoth, as one who has attained the Great Work and stands ready to illumine all others below Him on the Path with the threefold teaching of the ages. Yet only those who are truly fit for His Teaching can recognize His Wisdom. The unfit cannot recognize His Wisdom, since they are blind and stupid, unable to see or comprehend the obvious, the Light that is even now upon them.)

30. Thou shalt also know that the Three Higher Principles of which We speak are mysterious revelations of a more Ineffable Trinity of Inscrutable Unity.

(*Comment:* This seems to imply a mystery of Qabalistic significance in which Kether, Chokmah and Binah are but reflections of three higher abstract concepts, called Ain [Nothing], Ain Soph [The Limitless], and Ain Soph Aour [The Limitless Light]. These are the three Veils of Negative Existence which are beyond the Tree of Life. From them, however, emanate the three Supernals, and from these the remaining Sephiroth.)

31. Now the Inward Work is threefold; and the Outward Work is threefold. Each is a Threefold Unity of Soul, Mind and Body.

(*Comment:* The Inward Work is, of course, Mystical Alchemy and the Outward Work is, of course, Sexual Alchemy. Both of these operations are comprised of three basic stages. These three stages are called Nigredo, Albedo and Rubedo, or the Black, the White and the Red. Nigredo is the stage of Dissolution, which is the Purification of our work; Albedo is Coagulation, which is the Synthesis of our work; and Rubedo is Sublimation, which is the Multiplication of our work.

These three stages are represented by three figures, which constitute the Astrological Trinity of Scorpio. These are the Scorpion, the Serpent, and the Eagle. The Scorpion is Nigredo, the Serpent is Albedo, and the Eagle is Rubedo. The latter of these three is the astrological equivalent of the alchemical Phoenix and Pelican. It represents the Great Attainment, the rebirth of the soul or stone, which can now transfigure all base metals into the Perfect Gold of Nature. Thus the great emblem of the New Order of Nature. Thus the great emblem of the New Order of the Golden Dawn is the Eagle whose Vast Wings represent the Liberty of the Adept to accomplish the Great Work.

The three stages of Mystical Alchemy, or the three states of the stone, are transmutations of a most peculiar kind.

They are, in fact, metamorphic in nature, constituting actual quantum jumps or abrupt transitions from one state of development to another; they do not necessarily follow a logical pattern of change. The stone itself remains continuous throughout the operation, but the changes it endures are not connected with each other in any phenomenological or observable sense. Each stage is a complete transformation of the stone, a veritable death and rebirth of its soul from one state of existence to another. Each stage, though it is the natural result of our work, comes about unexpectedly; it is an unpredictable event in the space-time continuum.

Now in this threefold experimental operation the saline stone of Our Majestic Work first undergoes a critical death or disintegration process, which is also a purification of its soul, mind and body. It then becomes the White Tincture of our work, which is a magical consecration of the stone, and this White Tincture transmute base metals into the Silver of the Moon. Then it becomes the Red Tincture of our work, the Elixir of Life, which transmutes base metals into the Living Gold of the Sun.

In Egyptian mythological symbolism, this threefold operation is represented by the slaying of Osiris by his brother Set, His revival through the Magick of His wife Isis, and His mysterious resurrection in His son Horus, who is the *Aurora Aurea* or Golden Dawn of Our Regal Art, and whose holy image is the Solar Eagle. Such is the death and rebirth of THAT which is like unto itself: such is the Great Experiment of the Royal Art of the Sun!

DISSOLUTION is the FIRST KEY to the GREAT WORK. It is the purification of Sulphur and Mercury.

COAGULATION, the second key, is the unification of Sulphur and Mercury withe aid of Salt. These two keys correlate with the alchemical formula "solve et coagula". SUBLIMATION, the third key, is the multiplication of the stone by repeating the actual operation, and the effect of this process is the exaltation of the Philosopher's Stone.

Eliphas Levi wrote in "Dogme et Rituel de la Haute Magie": *"This stone is both one and manifold; it is decomposed by analysis and recomposed by synthesis. In analysis it is a powder, the achemical powder of projection; before analysis and in synthesis it is a stone."* The analytical decomposition of the stone is the dissolution of our work; it is the volatilzation of the fixed. The synthetic recomposition of the stone is the coagulation of our work; it is the fixation of the violatile. These two alchemical processes result in the production of the Philosopher's Stone, but only in potential form. It is not until stone is subjected to Sublimation that it is completely regenerated and, ergo, capable of transmuting base metals into gold and conferring immortality.

Sublimation ultimately becomes an eternal self-generating process which regenerates the stone time and time again, making of the stone an immortal soul, and an eternal traveler on the Great Circle of Perpetual Initiation. Sublimation makes for the immortalization of the stone; it is the Principle of Eternal Change, the magical perpetuity of the stone, which constitutes its immortal existence. As the Greek philosopher Heraclitus once said: *"There is nothing permanent except change."*)

32. The Hidden Stone of the Ages is thus obtained, even here and now. Let the Sun and the Moon unite; let them bear

an Hermaphrodite! Let a child be born: it shall be the Stone of the Sages, the Medicine of Metals, and the Elixir of Life.

(*Comment:* It is by scientific application and execution of the threefold operation of Alchemy that the Stone of the Philosophers is to be obtained, here and now. The Sun is man; the Moon is woman; and the Hermaphrodite is the magical product of their union. This Hermaphrodite is Two-in-one; S/he is the Rebirth of the Sun and Moon. Such is called their Magical Child and is the Great Secret of Alchemy, the *Arcanum Arcanorum*, which constitutes our true power and wealth on earth, the key to our immortality and orderly perpetuation as an evolving species. The Magical Child is also known as the Stone of the Sages, Medicine of Metals, Universal Medicine, Elixir of Life, Universal Solvent, Dew of Immortality, Amrita, Soma, Mana, Eucharist of the Sun, Wine of the Sabbath, Power of Projection, Red Tincture, Unguent, Pill of Power, Potable Gold, and the Quintessence. Such is the mystery of Samson's Riddle: *"What is sweeter than honey, and stronger than a Lion?"* It is also the mystery of which Paracelsus wrote in "The Aurora of the Philosophers": *"The Son of Hamuel says that the Stone of the Philosophers is Water Coagulated, namely in Sol and Luna. From this is it clearer than the Sun that the matter of the Stone is nothing else but Sol and Luna."* In Michael Maier's "Chemical Secrets of Nature", it is written: *"The offspring of the Sun and Moon is the Philosopher's Red Stone, floating upon the liquid in the crucible."*

33. Also the Threefold Unity Above is expanded into a seven-petalled Rose; and on each petal there is inscribed in fire one of the seven letters of VITRIOL.

(*Comment:* Kether, Chokmah and Binah, in their subtle interplay of orgasmic ecstasy, produce seven other emanations or Sephiroth on the Tree of Life. These are Chesed, Geburah, Tiphareth, Netzach, Hod, Yesod, and Mulkuth. To these correspond the seven Metals of Alchemy, the seven Chakras of Yoga and the seven traditional Planets of Astrology. Such form a seven-petalled Rose with the letters VITRIOL inscribed in fire on its petals.

VITRIOL is a Notariqon for *"Visita Interiora Terrae Rectificando Invenies Occultum Lapidem"*, which is Latin for "Visit the interior parts of the earth; by rectification you will find the secret stone." VITRIOL is the name that Basilius Valentinus [Basil Valentine] applied to the Universal Solvent, a secret diluent salt. VITRIOL represents the balanced combination of Sulphur, Salt and Mercury. And how is this achieved? *"Make the fixed volatile – unite the fugitive male with the fixed female."*

Basil emphasized a third Principle in the Great Work which he called Salt, concerning which he wrote: *"Salt is the fire, the water that does not wet one's hands."* VITRIOL is a name for this third Principle; it is also a name for the Philosopher's Stone. In the word VITRIOL is contained the formula of the Great Work by which the Adept can attain the Secret Stone through the rectification of the salt and its subsequent regeneration.)

34. Also each rose petal is of a different color: four petals are mixed, and the other three are virgin. Also each petal has a unique scent, taste, and touch to it. All these come forth form the Centre of the Cross, that is, from the place of the Palace of the Stars in the midst of it all.

(*Comment:* Netzach, Hod, Yesod and Malkuth are impure; they are mixed principles, combinations of the interplay of Chesed, Geburah, and Tiphareth, which are reflections of Kether, Chokmah, and Binah. Colors pertain to sight, the sense of Fire. Scent is Air, taste is Water, and touch is Earth. These four elements are manifestations of the seven Sephiroth below the Abyss which come forth from the Center of the Cross of the Sun.

Note also that the Sevenfold System of Initiation in the New Order of the Golden Dawn [Thelemic Order of the Golden Dawn] there are four outer stages and three inner. The four outer stages are four gates to the Palace of the Stars in which we experience the Three Invisible Rites of Initiation. The completion of these seven stages of initiation makes for the attainment of THAT which exists beyond the Planetary Spheres; it constitutes the transcendence of the Planetary Spheres and the subsequent attainment of the Gnostic Ogdoad, which is the eighth sphere of Celestial Wisdom.)

35. And in each letter of fire on the seven petals of the Sacred Rose there is concealed a vision and a voice. And in each vision and voice there is concealed a divine splendour of unspeakable transmutations of ineffable mystery and wonder. All these inner splendours are different stages of Our Master Opus of Divine Transformation which can be interpreted in many ways in many lands.

(*Comment:* In each Sephira there is concealed a vision and a voice corresponding to its own particular nature. This is the vision and the voice of initiation. And in each vision and voice there is concealed a divine splendor which partakes of the nature of the initiation that corresponds thereto and which is capable of being interpreted and defined in a variety of ways.)

36. So saith Hermes Trismegistus, Lord of Our Royal and Sacerdotal Art of Alkhemi, who is also the Wisdom of the Gods and the Logos of the Ineffable Unknown. Mysteries revealed are mysteries concealed; and none but the Wise may decipher them. This Holy Book of the Magick of Hermes is hermetically sealed; and none but the Wise may unravel its sublime splendours of High Wisdom for the accomplishment of the Great Work of the Sun; yea, for the accomplishment of the Great Work of the Sun.

(*Comment:* In this holy book are many mysteries of Our Royal and Sacerdotal Art revealed by the Voice of the Logos Himself; but, it is a true saying: "*That which guides the Wise misleads the foolish.*" This holy book is sealed with the Spirit of Wisdom itself, and only the Wise may intuit and commune with that Spirit to attain the Great Work, the Summum Bonum, True Wisdom and Perfect Happiness.)

Hermes Trismegistus

ABRAHADABRA

666

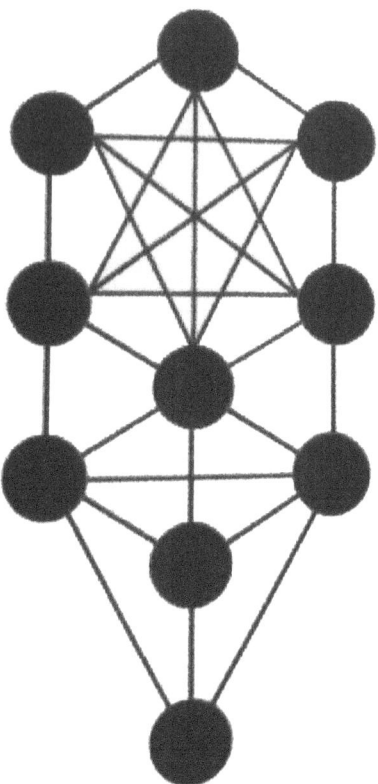

The Thelemic Tree of Life

THE QABALAH OF THE ANTICHRIST

English Qabalah: THE KEY OF IT ALL

By David Cherubim - *Quartus Cherub*
1996 e.v.

In Liber AL II:55, it is written in the Voice of our Lord Hadit: "Thou shalt obtain the order & value of the English Alphabet; thou shalt find new symbols to attribute them unto." The English Alphabet has 26 letters, whereas our traditional Magical Alphabet, the Hebrew Alphabet, has only twenty-two letters. The twenty-two letters of the Hebrew Alphabet are linked with the twenty-two Paths of the Qabalistic Tree of Life and with the twenty-two Atu of Thoth (Major Arcana of Tarot). The 26 letters of the English Alphabet also pertain to the twenty-two Paths which connect Sephiroth on the Qabalistic Tree of Life, and also to the four secret Paths of the Ageless Tree which also connect certain Sephiroth on the Tree. The order of the English Alphabet, as indicated in verse 55 of Chapter II of the Book of the Law, pertains to the proper arrangement of the 26 letters of the English Alphabet on the Qabalistic Tree of Life. Their value, as indicated in this same verse, denotes a new system of Numerology. The new symbols of this same verse denote the four secret Paths of the Tree of Life which, till this day, have remained hidden in the Sanctuary of the

Occult Wisdom. But the Tree of Life is incomplete without the addition of the four secret Paths, and therefore we must now expound upon these four Mysteries to make whole that which was partial.

The making visible of the four secret Paths on the Tree of Life gives birth to a new Tree to accord with the English Alphabet, which is our Magical Alphabet for the New Aeon of Horus. This new Tree of Life, which incorporates the English Alphabet of 26 letters rather than the 22 letters of the Hebrew Alphabet, gives us 36 Paths of Wisdom in all (10 Sephiroth and 26 Paths). The sum of the numbers of 36 is 666, the Great Number of the Sun. Also, 36 is the Mystic Number of the Sephira Hod or the sum of 8, which is the number of Thoth-Hermes-Mercury, the Logos or Word of the Gods, and the Lord of Magick, Occult Science and Tarot.

The 26 Paths of the new Tree of Life give us a new Major Arcana of Tarot, a set of "new symbols" or Trumps, which include four new Atu of Thoth, called "Knowledge, Courage, Will, and Silence" or "To Know, To Dare, To Will, and To Keep Silence." These are the four Powers of the Sphinx, which are the Occult Virtues of the initiated Magician. The four new Atu of Thoth are also linked with the four Worlds of the Qabalah (Atziluth, Briah, Yetzirah, and Assiah), the four Cherubim or Holy Living Creatures who guard the Universal Sanctuary of Wisdom, and the four Thelemic principles of Light, Life, Love and Liberty. They are also linked with the four Philosophical Elements of Fire, Water, Air and Earth, whereas the remaining twenty-two Trumps of Tarot correspond with Sol, Luna, the eight Planets (Pluto, Uranus, Neptune, Saturn, Jupiter,

Mars, Venus and Mercury) and the Twelve Astrological Signs (Aries, Taurus, Gemini, Cancer, Leo, Virgo, Libra, Scorpio, Sagittarius, Capricorn, Aquarius and Pisces).

The four mysterious Paths, like the common twenty-two Paths of the Tree of Life, connect two Sephiroth each. Thus one Path connects the two Sephiroth called Geburah and Chokmah, another Path connects Geburah and Kether, another Path connects Chesed and Binah, and another Path connect Chesed and Kether. From this it will be observed that a second unicursal Hexagram can be formed on the Tree of Life, with Da'ath in its center, whereas the first Unicursal Hexagram contains Tiphareth in its center. Also, a second Pentagram can be formed on the Tree of Life with the application of the four secret Paths. The four secret Paths complete the symbol of the Tree of Life, making it a perfect symbol of the Unity of All Things. These four paths make perfect that which was an imperfect image of the Universe, giving birth to a whole new Qabalistic system of classification and thinking.

26, the number of letters and paths in our Thelemic Qabalah, is the sacred number of the Tetragrammaton or Yod-Heh-Vav-Heh (IHVH). The Tetragrammaton corresponds with the Four Worlds of the Qabalah. Our English Qabalah contains the Mysteries of the Four Worlds. 26 is also the sum of the numbers of the Four Sephiroth of the Middle Pillar: 1 (Kether) + 6 (Tiphareth) + 9 (Yesod) + 10 (Malkuth) = 26. The Middle Pillar is a Phallic Symbol of the Yechidah (True Self) and it is the Great Key to Initiation. Our English Qabalah contains the Mysteries of Initiation. 26 is also the sum of the numbers of the four Fixed Signs of the Zodiac, that is, Taurus (2), Leo (5), Scorpio (8), and

Aquarius (11). These are the Cherubim, the Angels of the Elements from the point of view of Malkuth (Earth) or the Holy Living Creatures from the point of view of Kether (Spirit). These Holy Cherubim are magically linked with the four mysterious Paths on the new Tree of Life. They are the Angelic Guardians of the Sacred Mysteries, Four-in-One and One-in-Four, that is, the Fourfold Nature of the Winged Sphinx of the Sun.

26 is the magical number of the Cube of the Sun. It is written in the Book of the Law that the Cube is a symbol of our Lord Hadit, the Sun. The Cube has 6 sides, 8 points or corners, and 12 edges or boundary lines. The Cube contains the Great Secret of the Universe. In Alchemical terminology, it is the Stone of the Philosophers. The Cube is made of six squares; it is therefore lined with the Hexagram, the sacred symbol of the Sun. It is the Folded Cross of six square which contains the Mystical Rose or Pentagram in its Center. The Rose is concealed in the Cube or Folded Cross; it represents the Secret of Secrets or the *Arcanum Arcanorum* of our Sacred Magick. By the unfolding of the Cube of the sun is this Great Secret revealed; and the Cross and Rose, the Hexagram and Pentagram, become One in Eternity.

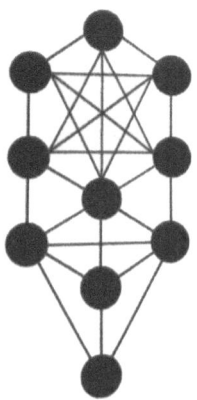

The Order & Value of the English Alphabet

The order and value of the English Alphabet is simple yet profound in nature. The order pertains to the Paths of the new Tree of Life, which are linked with the 26 letters of our Thelemic Alphabet. The value of each letter is a multiplication of Six, the sacred number of the Beast (The Sun). 26 multiplied by 6 produces the number 156, which is the sacred number of Babalon (The Moon). The English Alphabet is the Magical Alphabet of the Sun and Moon. The value of the English Alphabet begins with the number of the Beast (The Sun) and ends with the number of Babalon (The Moon).

Numbers and their Words by use of the English Qabalah

The proof of our system of the English Qabalah can, for the most part, be found in the successful application of the Science of Gematria, which is based on the relative numerical values of words. That is, words and/or phrases with the same numerical value can be related or linked with each other. For example, according to our system, the words English Qabalah produce the number 696, which is the number of Thelemites and Key of it All (AL III:47). The

English Qabalah is the Key of it All for Thelemites, that is, for those who accept the Book of the Law and Thelema. The word Thelema in our system produces the number 384. So does the word Nuit. Thus Thelema is equivalent to Nuit. And, as a final example, the words Ankh-af-na-khonsu, Ra-Hoor-Khuit, and Double Wanded One, all produce the number 864. This requires no comment. It is enough to say here that our system obviously works!

The words of our English Qabalah can also be linked with words from other systems through their equivalent numerical values. So, for instance, the Hebrew words ShMSh VIRCh (Sun and Moon) and AShT ZNVNIM (Woman of Whoredom) give us the numerical value of 864 in the Hebrew Qabalah. The Sun and Moon and Woman of Whoredom can therefore be related to the words Ra-Hoor-Khuit, Doubled Wanded One, ankh-af-khonsu, and Scarlet Woman, which all produce the number 864 by use of our English Qabalah. As another simple example, the word Babalon, by use of the Hebrew Qabalah, produces the number 156. By our system, the word God produces the number 156. We may thus freely interpret this as implying that Babalon (The Moon) and God (The Sun) are One. The possibilities are infinite!

As a final note, the following listed words are mainly English, Latin, Hebrew, Greek, Egyptian, Sanskrit, Chinese, Japanese, and Arabic. This list of numbers and words is by no means complete and can be expanded upon by the serious student of our English Qabalah of our English Qabalah. Many of the words listed below are from Liber Legis (The Book of the Law).

12 = A∴A∴.

18 = Ba, AB.

24 = Aba.

45 = Ah, Add.

60 = Aha.

66 = G∴D∴.

72 = Ka, Aib.

78 = had, AL, LA, He, Id, Age.

84 = Ida.

90 = O, Bal, Ama.

96 = Kaaba, Fade, Gi.

102 = Ob.

108 = Die, Deed.

114 = Egg, Ra, And, Adam, Jah, Od.

120 = Cabala, Abel, Kah, Nada, Anda, Chi, Ki.

126 = R∴C∴, AGLA, ABIDE, Li.

132 = Go, Abra, Lead, Bija, Kaia.

138 = Ho, Oh, I Am, Made, In, Kebad, Haha, Naga.

144 = Nia, Ain, Io, Aub, Aima.

150 = IAO, OAI, All, Sea, Bend, Mecca, Te.

156 = God, AL-LA, Ajna, Bare, Hide, Eat, Aud, Obi, Lam, Kama.

162 = Din, Ego, Cain, Lo, Red, Hand.

168 = OM, Japa, Man, Air, Dare, Eva, Hara.

174 = ON, AOM, Black, Asi, Isa, Chiah, Gog, Chela.

180 = Agape, Magi, Eagle, ABMN, HUA, Peace, Ye, Hail, Bible, Raja.

186 = Pan, Chief, Obeah, Odic, Kamea, Cube, Bell, Aye, Anicca, Agni, Kara.

192 = Life, Ire, Fate, Eve, Abased, Dew, Leo, Sage, Deva, Veda, Jihad.

198 = Name, Amen, Gate, Alas, Magic, Mara, Lil, Kali, Akasa, Kata.

204 = One, Kin, Allah, Camel, Binah, Daath, Grace, Lila, Vach, Kami.

210 = Nu, Aeon, Aum, Ananda, Lance, Pen, Peck, Eye, Flap, Bond, Image, Keen, Grade, Orb, Abbey, Nil, Maat, Lamed, Mahdi, Padma, China.

216 = Child, Tao, Law, F.I.A.T., Kaph, Oil, Come, Asana, Hari.

222 = Khem, Flame, Rod, Hex, Hell, Hades, Edom, Teach, Fold, Seal, Sela, Apas.

228 = Palace, Gold, Fire, Apep, Alpha, Ion, Briah, Bride, Ocean, Nigh, Death, Change, Anima, Bodhi, Hatha

234 = Angel, QBLH, ST (Set), Ass, Asar, Ox, Graal, Wicca, Cakes, Art, Albedo, Ibis, Hold, Engage, Vice, Laya, Loka.

240 = Khu, Robe, Aur, Mind, Maya, Devi, Buddha, Marga, Dhamma, Jnana, Yama, Chit, Sat, Madim, Us, Blue, Cup, Nile, Nay, HCOMA.

246 = Khabs, Akasha, King, Omega, Chalice, Key, Alien, Defile, Awake, Abaddon, Oz, Eloah, Pax, Koan.

252 = Hadit, Self, Coph, Aleph, Wand, Dagger, Cloak, Rebel, Charge, War, Budo, Odin, Qabalah, Atu, Arcane, Libra, Sin, Hecate, Tau, Math, Lamp, Chakra, Hum, Jiva, Agamas.

258 = Kiblah, Hawk, Ares, Mark, Tav, Charm, Cast, Tin, Adore, Book, Regal, Lodge, Goat, Magog, Guna, Aditi, Brahma, Mahat, Linga, Hansa, Bhakta.

264 = Magick, Oath, Karma, Godhead, Adonai, Set, Hidden, Space, Aum Ha, Yod, Chesed, Abraham, Opal, Gems, Cancer, Cheth, Dojo.

270 = Gods, East, Zen, Path, Enoch, Elijah, Ptah, Lamen, Leader, Ojas, Dharma.

276 = Wanga, Chant, Adept, Aurae, Aurea, Sol Anahata, Ogdoad, Magical, Liber, Link, Zraa, Khemi, Cairo, Exceed, Behold, Them, Chaos, Body, Dung, Dove, Hero, Shaddai, Elias, Indra.

282 = Beast, Babalon, Grail, Nemo, HRU, IHVH, Beliar, Alone, Monad, Time Ahephi, Anubi, Embrace, Ablaze, Force, Bull, Dharana, Jinn, Yang.

288 = Yoga, Tree, Ring, Son, None, Fool, Evil, Veil, Labor, Craft, Sex, Soma, Blood, Luna, Shu, Arhat, Buddhi, Manas, Yin.

294 = Lord, Deus, Way, Cause, Not That, Atom, Atman, Beetle, Ayin, Enigma, Sign, Athena, Rajas, Aikido.

300 = Chiefs, Circle, Sangha, Salem, Orgia, Joy, Sacred, Drug, Snake, Lion, Fohat, Bindu, Prana, Shin, Hyle, Ceres, Learn, I.N.R.I., Redeem, Flesh, Tomb, Fight, Animal, Wind, Voice, Owl, I Ching, Tai Chi, NANTA.

306 = Ta-Nech, Samuel, Khamael, Iblis, Siva, Mars, Falcon, Aureae, Demon, Go On, Feast, Wine, Elite, Rome, Fates, Task, Forge, Guard, Ruach, Michael, Yajna, Bhakti.

312 = Heru, Heart, Legis, Seth, Daemon, Pride, Devil, Tacere, Anpu, Altar, Earth, Guph, Salt, Rite, Mass, Pope, Six, Aries, Arise, Raise, Staff, Create, Door, Ordo, Madhya, Diksha, Vajra.

318 = N.O.X., To Me, Womb, Conceal, Many, Divide, Banish, Soar, Reign, Regis, Dhyana, Seti, Sabbath, Myo.

324 = Love, Vagina, Regina, Voice, Breath, Aeons, Eyes, Sun, Peacock, Oracle, Taro, Ator, Rota, Combat, Engine, Girt, Beware, Creeds, Audere, Scire, Gabriel, Islam, Tum, Tamas, Budoka.

330 = Satan, Io Pan, Ordeal, Anus, Samadhi, Aour, Sky, Heaven, Adepti, Sufi, Song, Girdle, Burn, Object, Ganesha, Ahankara.

336 = Hoor, Lingam, Semen, Light, Ether, Ardor, Iron, Will, Velle, Toil, Attack, Enflame, Isis, Wise, Scribe, Poet, Paper, Sigil, Bound, Yoke, Yogi, Karate.

342 = Abrahadabra, Magician, Magickal, Lux, To Go, Aught, Anatta, No Man, Cherub, Kerub, Mezla, Bacchus, Goetia, Diary, Refine, Human, Assiah, Eros, Rose, Swan, Moon, Divided, Gemini, Abjure, Slay, Army, Mudra, Meru, Acharya, Brahman, Tapas.

348 = Star, Zodiac, Angels, Radiate, L.V.X., Fenix, Science, Father, Gedulah, Vices, Evoke, Night, Kiss, Emerald, Advaita.

354 = Liber AL, Cipher, Island, Keph-Ra, Brass, Spear, Shiva, Dragon, Thebes, Chokmah, Hagios, Alkhemi, Aryan, Koran, BITOM.

360 = Aiwaz, Akrasia, Word, Vow, Battle, Kings, Mingle, Pelican, Saladin, Teacher, Nakhiel, Inner, Order, Holy, Diamond, Pure, Desire, Pray, Hymn, Khut, Pekht, Pingala, Prajna, Aditya, Ashram, Seiza.

366 = Stele, Magus, Vox, The Man, Aquila, Thor, Steel, Raphael, Trance, Bliss, Chakras, Svara.

372 = Ompehda, Lurk, Amenti, Tuat, Concealed, Refuge, Queen, Riches, Delicacy, Climax, Amrita, Axiom, Action, Mason, Geburah, Nechesh, Elohim, Torah, Nyima, Dhammapada.

378 = Eleven, Yechidah, Penis, Yoni, Witch, Reveal, Divine, Avatar, Fiery, Sight, Know, Factor, Aright, Olive, Rishi, Sempai.

384 = Thelema, Nuit, Orbit, Paths, Tzaddi, Kteis, Bosom, Zero, Dust, Unit, Iacchus, Ahriman, Bright, Leaping, Red Flame, Censer, Musk, Spit, Spell, Test, Cower, Push, Thou, Wilt, Cometh, Depart, True, Chosen, Vehicle, Zion, Israel, Qadosh, Vital, Mercy, Amoun, Dikshaka, Avatara, Kriya, EXARP.

390 = Center, Hoori, Armies, Red Gleam, Rejoice, Solar, Delight, Enchant, Music, Orgy, Caress, Breast, Attain, Mental, State, Beyond, Prince, White, Horse, Alphabet, Choose, Method, Token, Rubedo, Arjuna, Shambala.

396 = Coph Nia, ALGMOR, Abrasax, Abyss, Black Flame, Freedom, Blessed, Lunar, Woman, Curse, Smite, Swear, Stir, Beasts, Upon, Floor, Ruby, Rich Man, Single, Empire, Sodom, Anubis, Auriel.

402 = Kheph-Ra, Kether, The One Silence, Alchemy, Ishmael, Male Child, Honey, Water, West, Hanged Man, Vesta, Hegemon, The Fine, Soul, Challenge, Work, Cabalist, Mantra, Moksha, Guru.

408 = Logos Hermes, Shakti, House, Planet, ARARITA, Aspire, Praise, Poetic, Mirth, Frater, Helios, Melekim, Manus, Genital, Pillar, Decipher, Zohar, Heretic, Avesta, Karateka.

414 = Khuit, Reward, MUAUM, Jasper, Emblems, Nous, Orphic, Knight, Kerubic, Archangel, Enochian, Mithra,

Enjoy, Serve, Whore, Akolasia, Coiling, Venom, Drugs, Joys, Wealth, Dynamic, Paradigm, Abrogate, People, Vayu.

420 = Secret, Proof, I am Alone, Galaxy, Azoth, Metals, Pour, Essence, Erotic, Feasts, Especial, Duty, Honor, Courage, Wrath, Bewitch, Enemies, Accuser, Lilith, Demeter, Israfel, Dzyan, Isvara, Yogin, Himalaya.

426 = Thoth, Virgo, Sperm, Royal, Temple, Astral, Sphere, Secure, Opus, Naught, Desert, Against, Purged, Arcanum, Spices, Jasmine, Ameshet, Apollo, Zeus, Pisces, Chakshu, Mahatman, Sensei.

432 = Bahlasti, Aiwass, Shaitan, Avenger, Warfare, Reguli, Lover, Marriage, Lust, Liberate, Nuith, One Palace, Neschamah, World, Samsara, Amulet, Pantacle, Money, Reason, Revealed, Siddhis, Nigredo, Mohammed, Krishna, Hanuman.

438 - LAShTAL, Hermit, Ophite, Crown, All in All, Union, Stone, Copper, Shrine, Perfect, Goddess, Crucible, Orgasm, Sacrifice, Paradise, Redeemer, Crafty, Fighter, Wotan, Mentu, Orus, Utchat, Egypt, Children, United Nation, Solve, Assuage, Anoint, Skry, Pranava, Samyama, Lakshmi.

444 = Lucifer, Messhiah, Aurora, Aurum, Solis, Proud, Martial, Beauty, Orgone, Energy, Severe, Ordeals, Weapon, Chariot, Tarot, Tantra, Occult, Element, Cross, Point, Quanta, Harlot, Accursed, Fruit, English, Gematria, Jewels, Jesus, IHShVH, He-Phren, Themis, Mukti.

450 = Ra-Hoor, Thelemic, Abuldiz, Iunges, Write, Eternal, Guardian, Electric, Genius, Eye of Ra, Abramelin, Templi, Ishtar, Direful, Profane, Shells, North, Friends, Arrow, Zayin, Yi King, Karate-Do.

456 = Behemoth, Belarion, Master, Bowels, Vault, Invoke, One Self, Highest, Revenge, Vengeance, Age of War, Jissen Absolve, Mongol, Diamanos, Psyche, Sephira, Musick.

462 = Chief of All, Chief Adept, Stars, New Aeon, Red Circle, Red Lion, Elixir, HRILIU, Diabolos, Christ, Hexagram, Shemesh, Caduceus, Athanor, Alkahest, Animus, Swift, Matter, Power, Glory, At Rule, Despise, Runes, Jivanu, Varuna.

468 = Scarlet, Red Wine, Mulier, All is All, Ars Regia, Lofty Genitalia, Nephesch, Slaves, Wage War, Bushido, Comrades, The Elect, Garment, Samkhya.

474 = Ordeal x, Sword, Kerubim, Cherubim, Nirvana, Baptize, Silent, Virgin, Love All, Gluten, Soften, Mother, Nature, Muladhara, Thrill, Arouse, Words, Tahuti, Kerux, Lao Tze, Sutra, Yantra.

480 = Baphomet, The Beast, Heru-Ra-Ha, Hawk's Head, Egg of Blue, Throne, Fellatio, Baptism, Subject, Girders, Kung-Fu.

486 = Horus, Augoides, Sorath, Elagabalus, Extended, Square, Tower, Ferment, Black Earth, Venus, Senses, Ritual, Wizard, Dikshita, Orient, Wu Wei.

492 = Soldier, Samurai, Armageddon, Basilisk, Strike, Ain Soph, Satori, Buddhahood, Man-Sun, Magical Child,

innocence, Quest, Rainbow, Qesheth, Anointed, Tongue, Myrrh, Sexual, Vessel, Pylon, Mighty, Intent, Rishis.

489 = Gnosis, Wisdom, Tehuti, Phallos, Motto, Magick Art, Splendid, Spells, Geomancy, Prayer, Comment, South, Forest, Black Sun, Adam Qadmon, Bodhidharma, Sattva, Dharmakaya, Bhagavad Gita.

504 = Apophis, Pluto, Lucifuge, Savior, Cosmos, Cucurbite, Convey, Particle, Perfume, Colour, Astarte, Daughter, Surya, Vajradhara, Taoist, Mushin.

510 = Hiereus, Enterer, Shemsu, Uraeus, Matrix, Nought, Tantric, Coition, Coagulate, Devour, Het-Heru, Hathoor, Soror, Vesper, Silver, Shroud, Curses, Fearless, Trample, Crucify, Golgotha, En to Pan, Kula Marga, Shinto.

516 = Mantras, Voodoo, Armour, Tantrica, Maha-Rishi, Brother, Adeptus, Knower, Revealer, Red Dragon, Celestial, Insight, Pyramid, Triangle, Formula, Conjure, Infinite, Motion, Loathing, Swoon, Libertas, Occidental, Mundum, Malkuth, Ahathoor, Sumeria, Nephilim, Sahasrara.

522 = No-Thing, Gnostic, Priest, Initiate, Sufism, Blessing, Coitus, Truth, All is One, Stellar, Planets, Perdure, Homeward, Pillars, Unique, Elemental, Lotus, Sruti, Kali Yuga.

528 = Khonsu, Purple, Excellence, Apostle, Mithras, Vision, Black Dragon, Vishudda.

534 = Therion, Phallus, Osiris, Amalantrah, Religion, Unity, Mystic, Success, Availest, Talisman, Hologram, Seriphim, Brahma-Dvara, Go-No-Sen.

540 = Orison, Sphinx, Alchemist, Inspire, Inmost, Emperor, Free Will, Thunder, Consume, Daimonos, Pranayama.

546 = Phoenix, Spirit, To Will, Liberty, Lovely, Darkness, Crimson, Sanctum, Sodomy, Chancellor, Ko Yuen.

552 = Boleskine, Leviathan, Magister, Sex Magick, Magical Link, Astrum Sapphire, Ecstasy, Vigour, Laughter, Confound, Nations, Numbers, Stones, The Seeing, Beni Elohim, Hermits, Ophites, Electron, Emanation, Yeheshua, Maitreya, Siddhartha.

558 = Strive, Conquer, Lifted Up, Solaris, Strong, Passion, Revealing, Saturn, Elements, Spangles, Pentalpha, Manipura, Vishnu.

564 = Sacrament, Paroketh, Uranus, Minerval, Covenant, Grimoire, Third Eye, Unicorn, Esoteric, Harmony, Good Ones, Oriental, Ahura-Mazda, Sannyasa, Mokuso.

570 = Clear Light, Pentagram, Dominus, Lord of All, Son of God, Solar Eagle, Sirius, Mazloth, Metagalactic, Manhood, Kundalini, Scorpio, White Eagle, Empress, Neptune, Purify, Process, Reverence, Nemyss, Gomorrah.

576 = Set-Heru, Bes-Na-Maut, War Engine, Metaphor, Knowledge, Freemason, Our Lady, Aphrodite, Overcome, Destiny.

582 = Thelemite, Zelator, Cake of Light, Delicious, Pleasure, Adoration, Blue and Gold, Serpent, Tempter, Angel of Hell, Protect, Sanctify, Holy Place, Electrum, Egyptian, Kinfolk, Fourfold, Cherubic Man, Capricorn, Sumeru.

588 - Prophet, Chosen One, Liber Legis, Militant, Age of Thelema, Regenerate, Typhon, Sacerdotal, Ceremony, Teletarchae, Proton.

594 = Golden Dawn, Holy Graal, Integrate, Fortify, Magickal Self, Conspire, Current, Firmament, Most High, God of Jupiter, Fortune, Vocation, Physics, Poetry, Letters, Olive Oil, Arduous, Rapture, Autocrat, Servant, Thought.

600 = Set-Hoor, Hrumachis, Perdurabo, Be Strong, Rituals, Benediction, Writing, Hermetics, Lithe Body, Macrocosm, Great Enigma, Lightning, Red Stone, Taurus, Vishudhi.

606 = Man of Earth, Shameless, Blasphemy, Evil Ones, Starry, System, Tree of Life, Invisible, Archetype, Kabeshunt, Nirvanin, Sunyata.

612 = New Order, Mystical, Warrior, Amorous, Perdurable, Sublimate, Unguent, Equation, Solstice, Orpheus, Svastika, Prakriti, Tao Te Ching.

618 = Great Rite, Consecrate, Princess, Alostrael, Student, Magical Diary, Androgyne, Mercury, Swastika, Sorcery, Intrigue, Politic, The Just, Pax Romana.

624 = Holier Place, City of God, Statue, Force and Fire, Eucharist, Substance, Arcanorum, Grand Word, Theurgy, Art of Magick, Evocation, Sandalphon, Bornless, Observer, Keep Silent, Elder Kings, Sunoches, Jerusalem, Purusha.

630 = V.I.T.R.I.O.L., Dissolve, Fire and Blood, Clitoris, Tiphareth, Equinox, Masonry, Brothers, Triumph, Joyous, Liberation.

636 = Infinity, True Self, Blood of a Child, Sphynx, Metatron, Bridegroom, Collective, Solar King, Prophecy, Masked Ones, Space-marks, Breed Lust, Rhapsody, Withdraw.

642 = Solar Self, Sun of Life, Brahmarandhra, Minister, Autocracy, Treasure, Mountain, Dance of Shiva, Quantum, Neutron, Aquarius, Tumautef.

648 = Locked Glass, Neophyte, The Profane, Microcosm, House of Ray, Worship, Secret Fire, Prime Agent, Green Dragon, Instinct, Jivamukta.

654 = Threshold, Royal Road, Metagalaxy, Seed of Satan.

660 = Love of Nu, Rosae Rubeae, Pure Joy Spirits, Nehushtan, Hermanubis, Apollyon, Practicus, Tincture, Royal Art, Meditation, Tao Teh King.

666 = Christos, Solar Adept, Sun-Kerub, Babe of Baphomet, Demiurgos, Strength, Perfection, Law of Love, Mystos, Noumenon, Emanations, Secret Key, Buttocks, Abramelin Oil, Computer, Autocratic, Angel of Mars, Inner Demon, Witchcraft, Necromancy, The Gross, Prithivi.

672 = Upon them, Curse Them, Victory, Fresh Fever, Lord of War, Rich Jewels, Veiled Sky, Yetzirah, Four Gates, Pure Heart, Unknown, Divinity, Upanishads.

678 = Night Sky, Universe, Ruach Elohim, All is Holy, Synergy, English QBLH, O Chosen One, O Prophet, Blessed Beast, Elohim Gibor, Flashing Flame, Strike Hard, Exorcist, Unveiling, Abomination, Apocalypse, Salvation.

684 = Hierophant, Inner Voice, Conquest, Desolation, Promises, Skew-wise, Folk folly, Perpetual, Giver of Life, Yin and Yang.

690 = Ra-Hoor-Khu, Initiator, Imperator, Khabs Am Pekht, Palace of Light, House of God, Middle Pillar, Agelong Love, A Little Child, Age of Horus, Eye of Shiva, Sulphur, Strategy, Intelligence, Certainty, Watchword, Nephthys.

696 = English Qalabah, Key of it All, Thelemites, Blind Nothing, Pure Will, Glorious, Angel of Light, Eternity, Sushumna, Vivasvat, Sannyasin.

702 = Prophets, Chosen Ones, Child Horus, Christus, Eternal Self, Atziluth, Position, Astral Body, Clerk-House, Communion, Divination.

708 = Great Work, Alchemystic, Unicursal, Limitless, Sephiroth, Theoricus, Fierce Lust, Wonderful, Cancellarius, Coagulation, Our Chosen, Servants, Thoughts, Incarnation.

714 = Hawk-Headed Lord, All Seeing Eye, High Priest, The Knower, Crown of All, Foundation, Frankincense.

720 = Secret Chiefs, Illuminati, Aurora Aurea, Aeon of Thelema, Heru-Pa-Kraat, Inner Teacher, Inner Order, True Will, Intention, Initiation, Incantation, Throne of Ra, Fortress.

726 = Child of Thelema, Strangely, Antichrist, Second Coming, Bodhisattva, Firstborn, Silent Self, Great Secret, Ecclesiastical, Revelation, Seven Seals, Law of Thelema, Lift thine Head, Rich Headdress.

738 = RPSTOVAL, Star of Space, Kerubic Sun, Severity, Conquering, Circumference, Five Senses, Joy of Earth, Means and Means, Conspiracy.

744 = Hoor-Pa-Kraat, Harpocrates, Splendour, Subtlety, Autonomy, Angra Mainyu, Goat of Mendes, Son of Satan, Star Ruby, Aureae Crucis, Prima Materia, Fire and Water, Conjunctio, Compassion.

750 = Aurora Aureae, Aurum Aureae, Solar Order, One Spirit, Aeon of the Child, Nuit and Hadit, Spiritual Mystery, Astral Sun, Unseen Force.

756 = Wormwood, Dionysus, Numinous, Lord of Light, Hierophantic, Conqueror, The Strong.

762 = Queen of Space, Circle of Light, Astral Light, Star and Snake, Laboratory, Altar of Love, Sacrificial Flame, Resurrect, Innermost, Oversoul.

768 = Choronzon, Emblems of Death.

774 = Lord of Thebes, Blazing Star, Stellar Self, Intimate Fire, Love of Will, Hierosgamos, Magick of Thelema.

780 = Babe of the Abyss, Infinite Space, Priestess, Secret Word, Three Ordeals, Rosicrucian, Sun and Moon, Elixer of Life, Drunkeness.

786 = Rose Cross, Rosae Crucis, Crucifixion, Illuminism, Sun of Light, Inner Temple, Intuition, Transmute, Alchemystical, Paradigm Shift.

792 = Prophet of AL, Chosen One of AL, Prophet of Had,

Globed Priest, Sun of Assiah, Lux Occulta, Astrology.

798 = Solar Logos, Konx Om Pax, Palace of the King, Cross of Gold, Visible Object.

804 = Serpent Flame, Force of Coph Nia,

810 = Ra-Hoor-Khut, Secret Centre, Circle Squared, Sublimation, Exceed by Delicacy, Rich Garments.

816 = Fire and Sword, Consecration, Fraternity.

822 = Eye of Horus, Cube in the Circle, Divine Element, Red Tincture, Chaioth ha Qadosh, Shemsu Heru, Lord of Silence, Child of the Beast, Child of Baphomet, Capricornus, Zoroaster.

828 = Queen of Heaven, Kisses of Nu, Host of Heaven, Lapis Lazuli, Synthesis, Ouroboros, Ropstoval, Spirit of God, Lord of Lords, Man in the Sun, Hierophantes.

834 = English Alphabet, Four Cherubim, Preterhuman, Anointed Cherub, Sun of Nuit, Son of Thelema, Thunderbolt.

840 = Magnum Opus, Hermaphrodite, Prometheus, Conjuration.

846 = Purification, Tribulation, False Prophet, Reincarnation, Relativity, Quantum Leap, Flaming Sword, Foursquare, Secret Temple, Starry Blue.

852 = Astron Argon, Ankh-f-n-khonsu, Forth-Speaker, Eagle of Liberty, Angel of the Lord, Novus Homo,

Abstruction, Rich Fresh Blood, Primus Agens, Silver and Gold, Astral Temple.

858 = Hoor-Paar-Kraat, Invisible Self, Immortal Self, Starry Self, Silver Star, Star of Nuit, Beauteous One, Eye of the Sun, Adeptus Major, Sanctification, Virgin's Milk, Cunnilingus, House of Tum.

864 = Ra-Hoor-Khuit, Double Wanded One, Ankh-af-na-khonsu, Prophet of All, Chosen One of All, Mark of the Beast, Sagittarius, Scarlet Woman, Rose of Ruby, Menstruum, Great Magical Agent.

870 = The Unknown, Laboratorium, Flame of the Sun.

876 = Child of Therion, Secret Master, Fire of the Sun, Gold of the Sun, Eye of the Sky, Collective Mind, Enlightenment, Shakti and Shiva, Chymical Marriage, Manifestation, Quicksilver, Om Mani Padme Hum, Svadhistthana.

882 = Jasmine and Rose, New Symbols, Choose ye well, Sacred Serpent, Worshipper, Under the Earth.

888 = A Secret Glory, English Gematria, Aurum Solis, Isis Unveiled, Circle of Stars, Rise Up and Awake, Law of Liberty, Implicate Order, Orgone Energy, Solar Phallos, Collective Self, Divine Presence, Morning Star, Star of the Child, Conspirator, Putrefaction, Nebuchadnezzar.

894 = Lovely Star, Unit of Nuit, Son of Baphomet, Infinite Factor, First Matter, Axle of the Wheel, Holy of Holies, Kingdom of Heaven, Passionate Peace.

900 = Love is the Law, Rosy Cross, Quintessence, Holy Spirit, Lord of Hosts, Victorious, Warrior Lord, Sword of Mars, Sweet Words, Continuous, Revolution.

912 = Vault of Heaven, Rosenkreuz, Solar Initiate, Prince-Priest, Theban Warrior.

918 = Son of Midnight, Thou Availest, Circle in the Middle, Path of the Sun, Androgynous, Ipsissimus, Causeless Cause, Medicine of Metals, Four Elements, Strange Drugs, Night-blue Sky, Unconscious Zarathustra.

924 = Star-lit Heaven, Stars of Light, Autonomous, Creeping Things, Beetle of Midnight, Prophet of Nu, Chosen One of Nu, Star of Ra-Hoor, Solar Phallus.

930 = Antichristos, Lord of the Earth, Sun of Baphomet, Beast of the Sun, Number of the Man, Fallen Angels of God, Starry Eyes, My Chosen Ones, Adeptus Minor, Knowledge of Death, Immortality, Firmament of Nu.

936 = Solar Spirit, Leaping Laughter, Burning Hearts, Purple and Green, House of Khephra.

942 = Star of the East, Fourfold Word, Way of the Sun, Business Way, Contemplation, Dissolution.

948 = Holy Chosen One, Majesty of Godhead, Warrior of Nu, Strong in War, Floor of the Palace, Wine of the Sabbath, Solve et Coagula, Philosophus.

954 = Sun of Midnight, All is not aught, Seed in the Metals, Blood of the Moon, Redintegration, Nosce te ipsum, Union with God, Twenty-Six, Sixfold Secret.

960 = Enginery of War, Labor of Hercules.

966 = Antichristus, Initiating Lord, Lord of Liberty, The Law is for All, Word of Baphomet, Mount Abiegnus.

972 = Blue-lidded Daughter, High Priestess, Miracle of Miracles, Oil of Vitriol.

978 = Infinite Stars, Company of Heaven.

984 = Scarlet Concubine, Worship of Nu, Love and Liberty, Spirit of Heru, Cult of the Sun.

990 = Kings of the Earth, Eyes of the Night, Worshippers, Secret Ardours.

1002 = Magister Templi, Quantum Jump, Sword in my Hand, Dragon of the Sun, Secret Serpent, Eternal Ecstasy.

1008 = Stella Matutina, Order of the Sun, Occultum Lapidem.

1014 = Winged Secret Flame, Particle of Dust, Choose ye an Island, Invisible House, Palace of the Stars, Sanctum Regnum, Seal of Perfection, Peace Unutterable, Grand Mystery, Wisdom of the Ages.

1020 = Power of Lust.

1026 = Avatar of the Sun, Metamorphosis.

1032 = Love under Will, Coiled Splendour.

1038 = There is success, Apostle of Thelema, Alphabet of the Sun.

1044 = Limitless Light, Serpent Power, Holy Guardian Angel, Quartus Cherub, Foursquare Name, Thelemic Golden Dawn, Lords of the Earth.

1050 = Stele of Revealing, Azure-lidded Woman, Arcanum Arcanorum, Mass of the Holy Ghost, Circumambulation, House of Ahathoor.

1056 = Milk of the Stars, Little Flowers, Joy of the World, Spirit of Nuit.

1062 = Spermatozoon, Hell's own Worm, Eye in the Triangle, Archangel of the Sun, Prince of Darkness, Antichristiandom, Push thy Order, Hierophantic Task, Unimaginable Joys.

1068 = Supreme Ritual, To Hell with them, One cometh after him, Stone of the Sages.

1074 = Blood of the Red lion, No expected House, Temple of the Sun, Hidden and Glorious, Son of Perdition, Lift up thyself, Crown of Creation, Spiritual Sun, That which remains.

1080 = Dominus Liminis, Red Circle in the Middle, Secret of Secrets, Sun of Tiphareth.

1086 = Kingdom of the Sun, Victory and Joy.

1092 = Heart of the Master, Inner Sanctuary, Light of the World, Fruit of the Sun, Star-Spendour, Excellent Kisses, Strike hard and low.

1098 = Universal Medicine, Stone of the Wise, Five Pointed Star, Rose of the World, Sepher Yetzirah.

1104 = King among the Kings, Lapis Mercurius.

1110 = Four Keys of Magick, Kerubim of the Earth, Fire-Water-Air-Earth, Ultimate Sparks.

1116 = Child of thy Bowels, Grave Mysteries, Matter in Motion.

1122 = Twin Warriors, Warrior of Thelema, Spirit of Ra-Hoor, Smite the Peoples, Three Ordeals in One, A Word not known.

1128 = Child of the Prophet, Age of the Antichrist.

1134 = Winged Snake of Light, Warrior-Priest, Knights of Baphomet.

1140 = One to follow thee, Numbers and Words.

1146 = Astrum Argentum, Pinnacles of Power.

1152 = Spirit of Baphomet, Son of the Morning, From right to left.

1158 = Praemonstrator, Mother of Harlots.

1164 = Centre of Pestilence.

1170 = Key of the Rituals, Three Grades of Thelema, Battle of Conquest, Lofty Chosen One, Bornless Spirit, Core of every Star, Priest of the Sun, Initiate of the Sun, Unicursal Hexagram.

1176 = Deal hardly with them, With Fire and Sword.

1182 = Minutum Mundum, Quadrature of Circle.

1188 = Drink Sweet Wines, Talk not overmuch.

1194 = Do What Thou Wilt, Spirit of the Sun, Antichristianity, Prophet of the Beast, Prophet of Baphomet, Hierophant of Thelema, Serpent of the Tree, Lust and Worship.

1200 = Numbers of the Sun, Perpetual Motion.

1206 = Girders of the Soul.

1212 = From Gold forge Steel, Star of the Morning, Starry System.

1218 = Great Work of Thelema.

1224 = Equinox of the Gods, Trees of Eternity.

1230 = God of War and Vengeance, As brothers fight ye.

1236 = Mountain of Abiegnus, Prophet of the Sun.

1242 = There are Love and Love, Miracle of the One Thing.

1248 - Thou shall reveal it, Victorious City, Legions of the Living, Joy of my Rapture.

1254 = Adeptus Exemptus, Refine thy Rapture.

1260 = Warrior of the Sun, Proof to the World, Squaring of the Circle, Stone of Eternity.

1272 = Lord of the Threshold, Sword of the Kerubim,

Inmost Sanctuary, Eucharist of the Sun.

1278 = Queen of Infinite Space, Kisses of the Stars, Knights of the Temple, Pillars of the World.

1284 = Transpersonal Self.

1290 = Priestess of Nuit.

1296 = City of the Pyramids, Lord of the Universe, Christeos Luciftias, Hierophant of Horus, Victorious Armies, Swell with my Force, Spiritum Sanctum, Uttermost Delight, Miraculous Colour.

1302 = Tribulation of Ordeal.

1308 = Arrow of Aspiration.

1314 = Four Gates to One Palace.

1320 = House of the Prophet, Child of the Sun and Moon.

1326 = Hawk-Headed Mystical Lord, System and System, Interior Universe.

1338 = Surpass the Stars, From top to bottom.

1344 = Crowned and Conquering, Sword of the Spirit, Uplifted in thine Heart.

1350 = Priest of the Princes.

1356 = Write sweet words, Great Work of the Sun.

1362 = Secret Fourfold Word.

1368 = Empress and Hierophant, Joy of Dissolution, Gluten of the White Eagle, Universal Solvent.

1374 = Stooping Starlight, Strive ever to more.

1386 = Warrior Lord of Thebes, Supreme and Terrible God, Apo Pantos Kako Diamanos.

1392 = The Slaves shall Serve, Mother of Abominations.

1398 = Logos of Ra-Hoor-Khuit, Star of the Antichrist, Spirit of Antichrist, Light-Life-Love-Liberty, Know-Dare-Will-Be Silent, Philosopher's Stone.

1404 = Reward of Ra-Hoor-Khuit, Prophet of Ra-Hoor-Khu, Chosen One of Ra-Hoor-Khu.

1410 = Winners of the Ordeals x, Trample down the heathen.

1416 = Chance shape of the letters.

1422 = Stop as thou wilt.

1440 = Success is thy Proof, Powers of the Sphinx.

1446 = Omnipresence of my Body, Purple beyond Purple, Priestess of the Moon.

1452 = Lighten the way of the Ka, Lapis Philosphorum, Splendour and Rapture, Existence is Pure Joy.

1458 = Unassuaged of Purpose, Vigour of your Arms, Abide with me Ra-Hoor-Khuit.

1464 = Great White Brotherhood, Discover the Key of it all, Soften and smooth down.

1470 = Open the ways of the Khu.

1476 = Temple of the Antichrist.

1482 = Let Blood flow to my Name.

1488 = Enterer of the Threshold, Abomination of Desolation.

1494 = Novus Ordo Seclorum, Temple not made with hands.

1500 = Nuit! Hadit! Ra-Hoor-Khuit!

1512 = Light higher than eyesight, Spirit of the Primal Fire.

1524 = Temple of the Holy Ghost, Conjuration of the Four.

1536 = Division hither homeward.

1554 = Sanctuary of the Gnosis, Rosae Rubeae et Aureae Crucis.

1560 = Crowned and Conquering Child, Fresh fever from the skies.

1572 = Visible Object of Worship.

1578 = Girt with a Sword before Me, Courage is your Armour.

1620 = None shall stand before you.

1626 = Minister of Hoor-Paar-Kraat.

1650 = Continuity of Existence.

1656 = Spirit-Fire-Water-Air-Earth.

1668 = Prince of the Power of the Air, Circle squared in its failure.

1674 = Mystery of Mysteries.

1680 = Lurk! Withdraw! Upon them!

1686 = Blue-lidded Daughter of Sunset.

1710 = Law of the Battle of Conquest.

1716 = Stones of Precious Water.

1722 = Stone of the Philosophers.

1746 = Secret of Perpetual Motion.

1770 = Voluptuous Night-sky.

1782 = Warrior-Priest of the Sun.

1806 = Prophet of the Lovely Star.

1818 = Lust and Worship of the Snake.

1884 = Raise the Spell of Ra-Hoor-Khuit, Unity uttermost showed.

1890 = With Swords and with Spears.

1920 = Lord of the Hosts of the Mighty.

1938 = Love is the law, love under will.

1962 = Priestess of the Silver Star.

1980 = Inspired forth-speaker of Mentu.

2004 = Infinite Possibilities of Nuit, Pleasure of uttermost delight.

2034 = Lightening the girders of the soul.

2118 = Direful judgements of Ra-Hoor-Khuit.

2124 = Dung it about with Enginery of War.

2148 = I am the Lord of the Double Want of Power, Hawk-Headed Lord of Silence and Strength.

2208 = Ultimate Sparks of the Intimate Fire.

2232 = Enjoy all things of sense and rapture.

2478 = There is no law beyond Do what thou wilt.

2664 = Do what thou wilt shall be the whole of the Law.

ABRAHADABRA

666

666

The Dark One is here,
A burning Lust within,
Destroying your restrictions
And illusions of sin.

Embrace his dark Love,
A sweet and bitter Kiss,
Beyond your little life,
A black flame of bliss.

The Dark One is come,
Not to betray,
But to free your Soul
And show you the Way.

His message is Freedom,
To do your Will,
That you may rejoice
And yourself fulfill.

The Dark One says:
We are all the Christ.
This is the true meaning
Of the Antichrist.

Antichrist is come,
Antichrist is here.
Do what you Will
With love and no fear.

I am Antichrist,
You are Antichrist,
We are all the Antichrist.

The Dark One is All,
The Many and the One,
A Universal Being
And a man in the Sun.

A Monster to many,
To others an Angel,
Rising from earth,
He's the Son of the Devil.

The Dark One says:
We are the Christ.
This is the true meaning
Of the Antichrist.

Antichrist is come,
Antichrist is here.
Do what you Will
With love and no fear.

I am Antichrist,
You are Antichrist,
We are all the Antichrist.

The Dark One is here,
A Spirit within all,
Lord of the World
And the Great Oversoul.

A Star from Beyond
With an All-Seeing Eye,
Looking from Earth,
Fire, Water and Sky.

His Eye is ablaze
With a great black Flame.
In a Triangle of Light
Is the Seal of His Name.

The Dark One says:
We are all the Christ.
This is the true meaning
Of the Antichrist.

Antichrist is come,
Antichrist is here.
Do what you Will
With Love and no fear.

I am Antichrist,
You are Antichrist,
We are all the Antichrist.

(Lyrics to the song 666 by David Cherubim, 2006)

ABOUT THE SCRIBE

David Cherubim was a musician, author, editor and occultist from Los Angeles, California. He performed and recorded as a solo artist, as well as with other artists. His song Thelema from his album BABALON (2007) was in the movie Abbey of Thelema (2008) about the world-famous occultist Aleister Crowley. He started and maintained the Aleister Crowley Foundation and the Thelemic Golden Dawn (which is influenced by the works of Aleister Crowley). He was an Adept of the Hermetic Golden Dawn (Israel Regardie lineage) and an Initiate of Aleister Crowley's Ordo Templi Orientis (O.T.O.). He is the author of *Alquimia: An Arte Negra (Alchemy: The Black Art*, Madras Editora, 1998) and contributed to various books published by New Falcon Publications, including *The Legend of Aleister Crowley* by Israel Regardie and P.R. Stephensen (Article co-written with Christopher Hyatt, 1990), *What you should know about the Golden Dawn* by Israel Regardie (Article, 1993), *Aleister Crowley and the Treasure House of Images* by J.F.C. Fuller and Aleister Crowley (Introduction, 2010), *Lucifer's Rebellion: A Tribute to Christopher S. Hyatt* (Article, 2011), and *The Eye in the Triangle: An Interpretation of Aleister Crowley* by Israel Regardie with an introduction by Robert Anton Wilson (Preface, 2011). He has proofread and edited various books for publication, including the following notable titles: *Rebellion, Revolution and Religiousness*, by Osho (Proofread Second Edition, 2010) *Ask Baba Lon* by Lon Milo DuQuette (Edited First Edition, 2011), *Enochian World of Aleister Crowley* by Lon Milo DuQuette (Edited Second Edition, 2011) and *What Does WoMan Want?* by Timothy Leary (Edited Third Edition, 2011).

New Falcon Publications
Publisher of Controversial Books and CDs
Invites You to Visit Our Website:
http://www.newfalcon.com

At the Falcon website you can:

- Browse the online catalog of all our great titles, including books by Robert Anton Wilson, Christopher S. Hyatt, Israel Regardie, Aleister Crowley, Timothy Leary, Osho, Lon Milo DuQuette and many more
- Find out what's available and what's out of stock
- Get special discounts
- Order our titles through our secure online server
- Find products not available anywhere else including:
    – One of a kind and limited availability products
    – Special packages
    – Special pricing
- And much, much more

Get online today at http://www.newfalcon.com